WATCH MY SMOKE

WATCH MY SMOKE

ERIC DICKERSON

WITH GREG HANLON

Haymarket Books
Chicago, Illinois

Published in 2022 by
Haymarket Books
P.O. Box 180165
Chicago, IL 60618
773-583-7884
www.haymarketbooks.org
info@haymarketbooks.org

ISBN: 978-1-64259-569-7

Distributed to the trade in the US through Consortium Book Sales and Dis-
tribution (www.cbsd.com) and internationally through Ingram Publisher Ser-
vices International (www.ingramcontent.com).

This book was published with the generous support of Lannan Foundation and
Wallace Action Fund.

Special discounts are available for bulk purchases by organizations and institutions. Please call 773-583-7884 or email info@haymarketbooks.org for more
information.

Cover photograph of Eric Dickerson before a National Football League game
in 1984 at Anaheim Stadium in Anaheim, California. (Photo by David Madi-
son/Getty Images)
Cover design by Eric Kerl.

Library of Congress Cataloging-in-Publication data is available.

10 9 8 7 6 5 4 3 2 1

CONTENTS

PREFACE

Bob Irsay staggered his drunk ass over to me and some of my Colts teammates.

It was 1990 or '91, and we were at the Christmas party he used to hold every year at his barn. Nobody ever wanted to go. Everybody knew Irsay, the Colts' owner, was a mean old alcoholic. We all had the feeling he was showing us off, as if he was saying, *Look at these big, Black bucks I have working for me.*

I was standing with wide receiver Clarence Verdin and a couple other guys when Irsay came over. His eyes were glassy. He was surrounded by two guys we called his "handlers." They followed him around everywhere to make sure he didn't say anything stupid that would get him in trouble. This time, they failed.

Irsay told us he had a joke.

—*You got a kike, you got a wetback, and you got a nigger...*

I didn't miss a beat. I'd known people like Irsay my whole life. My mom, Viola Dickerson, told me from an early age the country was full of them.

—*Fuck that,* I said.

The handlers tried to whisk Irsay away: *Bob, let's go, let's go.* Irsay snapped to his senses and began apologizing to us.

I repeated: *No, fuck that.* And I left that stupid party.

People wonder how Black athletes making millions of dollars can still feel used. People see us and think we're on top of the world, that somehow the racism that this country was founded on doesn't apply to us. Sometimes you can even convince yourself this is true. And then a guy like Bob Irsay walks up to you and your teammates—guys who beat the odds, guys who overcame obstacles most people couldn't imagine—and basically calls you a bunch of niggers.

The next day at the team facility, some management types called me into an office room, trying to smooth things over. They told me Bob was just joking, that he's not a racist, that *you know how he gets when he drinks.*

—*Yeah, yeah*, I told them. I wasn't stupid or born yesterday and I resented the implication that I was.

Maybe the organization was worried I was going to go public with it. But that thought didn't cross my mind. This was three decades ago and if there was such a thing as a "woke" media, it didn't exist in Indianapolis, as far as I could tell. This was the city where during a game fans hung a banner with a racist caricature of a Black baby in my number 29 jersey. He wore red lipstick and held a fried chicken leg in his hand, with a stack of money on one side and a watermelon on the other. This was the city where I flipped on the TV and saw a Klan rally in the middle of the downtown area. The news covered it like it was just another local organization having a parade.

So I left that office room and went to practice. There was another game coming up. More hits to take and more checks to cash.

The crazy thing was that the day after, Irsay probably didn't remember saying what he had said. But I never forgot it.

◆

This book is the story of my life. In a way, it's the classic American tale: A boy from the other side of the tracks in Sealy, Texas, goes to L.A. He becomes a star and makes the kind of money he never knew existed.

But it's also a darker tale about my conflicted relationship with football. About how I fell in love with the sport, but how by the end, all the bullshit surrounding it made me hate it.

How many of you know the feeling of running with the ball and breaking free into the open field when you're the fastest guy out there? I haven't played in twenty-eight years and I still can't get over it. The first time I felt it was in seventh grade, in my first organized football game. I was wearing prescription glasses because sports goggles weren't invented yet, and I scored six touchdowns. I chased that feeling ever since then, like an addict chasing the euphoria of that first hit.

I loved that feeling and everything associated with it, and still do. I love the way you *feel* the roar of the crowd when you're running for the end zone but you don't really *hear* it, because the only sounds you hear are your own breathing and the fluttering of your shoulder pads. I love the *smell* of the game. Every August, up until a few years ago, I'd still smell the game in the air when the season approached. That's how powerful of a hold it had on me.

I was lucky to get to chase that feeling for a living. I know what opportunities were like for Black kids from places like Sealy, and still are. God gave me a talent that was second to none. I have God and football to thank for the life I live today, and more importantly, for the life my kids live.

But then there's the bullshit.

The bullshit actually began way before I got to the pros. In high school, I quit the team temporarily because my coach was a racist who banned Afros and always worked the Black kids harder than the white kids. My senior year, after I got a certain Pontiac Trans Am—more on that later—I became the center of a scandal, like I was some kind of criminal. The NCAA came into town and started investigating me, my mom, and my grandma like they were the FBI.

The bullshit continued in college at SMU, with the "Pony Excess" scandal. Yeah, I got some envelopes of cash—and sent half that money back to my mom—and I always had a car to drive. But with the money I was making for SMU, that was peanuts. The real scandal isn't how *much* I got paid, it was how *little*. Forty years later, people think of the scandal and they think of me. You've been hearing a lot of talk these days about how society always assumes young Black men are criminals. Now, think back about the SMU scandal and how that was portrayed in the media—and who was portrayed as the wrongdoer.

Then there's the pros, when the ugly business of football takes over once and for all. You start to feel the brutality of the sport, and the way some people say that "NFL" stands for "Niggers for Lease." If you're an NFL running back, every time you touch the ball is like getting into a car crash. Now, at sixty-one years old, I feel those hits every second of every day in my body and, yes, in my mind.

And the money. Here's something people have a hard time understanding, and I can't really blame them: I might have been making more money than I ever thought possible, but that doesn't mean my contract was *fair* or even close to that. Nowadays, the media and fans are a little more tolerant of players' wanting their just due. But that wasn't the case in the '80s, before free agency, when the Rams underpaid me for years before eventually trading me.

To Indianapolis. Bob Irsay's team.

The trade broke my heart and hurts me still, because the Rams were the only team I ever wanted to play for. Do you think if a white guy broke the single-season rushing record and was in the middle of their prime as the best player at their position, they would've traded him? There's no chance in hell.

Of course, the media made me out to be the bad guy. *Eric the Ingrate*, they called me, a coded word if ever I've heard one. That's the way it was back then and nobody questioned it: the media, which was mostly white, took the side of management, which was also white, and the message got out to the fan base, which was also mostly white. There was no social media. My reputation was dictated by what they wrote about me.

But I'm not that guy at all. I'm a guy raised by strong, proud, loving parents to know right from wrong. I'm a guy who gave all he had to the game of football and paid the price. And that's why I decided to write this book.

CHAPTER 1

VIOLA & KARY

Sealy, Texas. When I was born in 1960, the population was 2,300. Even people who don't know Sealy as a town know the mattress company that was founded there. A dot on the map, fifty miles west of Houston. It's Texas, but in many ways it feels like the Dixie South.

The railroad tracks ran through town, Blacks on one side, whites on the other. Their streets were paved; I grew up on a dirt road. It was called Andrews Street when I was a kid but is now called Dickerson Street.

Racism was in the air we breathed, but it was subtle. Nobody ever called me the N-word, at least to my face. The town was so small that Black people and white people encountered each other all the time and got along, and kids of all races would play together. My elementary school was segregated, but then, with integration, we began attending middle school with the white kids, and it didn't seem like a big deal because we'd been around those kids our whole lives anyway.

Black people were second-class citizens, though. Nobody had to tell anyone that; it was just a fact of life. The houses in the white area were nicer. The Black elementary school I went to was smaller and shabbier. All of the cops were white and almost all of the professionals were too.

My dad worked for Southern Pacific Railroad and my mom cleaned houses on the white side of town. It was the classic case of *We were poor, but I didn't know it.* Unlike a lot of the kids I grew up around,

1

I lived in a stable and loving household. We didn't lack for food, necessities, or dignity. I never went to bed hungry or wondered where my next meal would come from.

My parents owned an acre and a half of land and had a nine-row garden with black-eyed peas, corn, cabbage, and some other crops. We were country, and thrifty: if we saw an armadillo dead by the side of the road, that was dinner. We'd shoot pigs between the eyes with a .22, then take them to our smokehouse out back. My dad would cut off the heads of chickens, and then I'd chase them down.

There wasn't much for us neighborhood kids to do. When we were little, we chased rabbits or played by the streetlight. When we got older, we'd race cars down the dirt roads, or have bonfires in the woods, or hang out by the 7-Eleven playing music and flirting. White, Black, it didn't matter. There wasn't any separation among us kids.

We'd see guys not much older than us on street corners, drinking. Some of them looked more strung out than others, and that's how we knew if a guy was also on drugs. Most of them were Black. We remembered when those guys had been teenagers a few short years ago. Everyone knew they didn't want to turn out like those guys. A lot of guys did anyway.

Sealy is famous for the mattress company, but its economy was mostly farming. There was also a steel plant and the railroad, my dad's employer. It wasn't a bad place to grow up, but I always knew I wanted something *bigger*. I didn't want my mom saying, *Yes ma'am, No ma'am* to a white lady much younger than she was, just because she cleaned her house. I wanted *nice things*. Like what my white friend Kevin Cubrick had. He lived in a two-story house with a bearskin rug, and his parents drove a Jaguar. My mom used to tell me that when I was a little kid, maybe five or six, I'd walk around our house saying, *I'm the king! I don't belong here!* I wanted more from life.

How I'd make that happen, I had no idea. I had no idea how good of an athlete I was. I didn't even know you could get paid lots of money for playing pro sports. But when I pictured myself as an adult, I didn't picture being in Sealy.

Because everyone in town knew: if you had big dreams, if you wanted to be somebody in this world, you were going to have to do it someplace else. That was especially true if you were Black.

•

My story begins like most people's stories: with my mom and dad.

My mom: Viola Dickerson. Biologically, she was actually my great-great-aunt. She was fifty-five years old when she adopted me as a toddler after my biological mom got pregnant with me when she was fifteen. I was close to my biological mom (birth name: Helen Shavers) but there was no doubt Viola Dickerson was my *mom*.

Everyone in the Black part of Sealy called her "Red" because they said she looked like an American Indian. She had wavy hair and light skin with freckles. She was what they used to call a "high yellow" back when she was growing up. The *yellow* referred to her skin color, to distinguish her from the darker Black people. The *high* referred to the social class her light skin was supposed to give her among Blacks, with the darkest people at the bottom. But she didn't see the world that way.

My mom was tough and firm and fierce but also loving, in a way that was often hard for me to see as a kid. She carried a gun at all times and cussed like a sailor, but she went to church every Sunday. She wasn't "sweet," but she was deeply moral. I can count on one hand the number of times she told me she loved me, but deep down, I never doubted she did. When she talked, I obeyed. If I didn't, I'd get the belt or the extension cord or whatever else she could get her hands on. To her, the world was a rough place, with no room for error, and she raised me with that in mind.

She was born in 1904 in Wallis, Texas, about twelve miles from Sealy, the daughter of a Black mother and a mixed-race father who drank hard and worked hard as a sharecropper. I never knew the full story of why my mom's dad was half-white, but when the topic came up, my mom would always say, *The white man will have his way with the Black woman.* I've always assumed my mom's grandmother was raped by a white man.

So, you can say that my mom's mistrust of white people ran through her blood. And then there were her life experiences. She was a generation older than my friends' parents, so she'd seen racism at its rawest and cruelest. She'd tell me stories of Black men she knew who'd been tarred and feathered. She'd seen a man strung up on a tree with his private parts stuffed into his mouth, all for the crime of *looking* at a white woman.

Sealy had changed a lot by the time I was growing up. Nobody was getting strung up on trees. In eighth grade, me and a white girl named Sheila Tomlinson liked each other, and it didn't seem like a big deal to me. But my mom wasn't having it.

—*There are two things that don't last long in this world*, she told me. *Dogs that chase cars and negroes that chase white girls.*

I listened because she knew what she was talking about. I listened because she was incredibly smart. She was really good with figures, especially money, and could multiply and divide things in her head in fractions of a second. She read a lot: I remember noticing as a kid that when she read a book out loud, she was so comfortable it was like she was just *talking*. She had been the valedictorian of her segregated high school class, and I always thought she'd make a great lawyer, or an accountant. But this was the 1920s in Texas, so there was no college and no career waiting for her. Instead, she spent her life cleaning white people's houses.

She never complained—she had no patience for people who complained or blamed other people for their circumstances—but I know the injustice ate at her. Her big thing was *fairness*. If something wasn't fair, if she saw someone getting over on someone else, she'd point it out. She wasn't gonna complain about the unfairness she experienced, but she didn't tolerate anyone else being treated unfairly.

Including me. I remember being eleven or twelve years old and trying out for Little League baseball. During tryouts, I hit three home runs. I could run, I could catch, I had a good arm. But after tryouts, they put me in the minor league, not the proper Little League. I was so shocked and hurt I started crying.

At that moment, I think my mom saw herself in me. Things had changed in Sealy, but in some ways they were still the same.

—*Eric, I'm telling you, even if you're two or three times better, sometimes it's just not enough,* she said. *I'm telling you, it's just different for us.*

♦

My mom came from a world where only the strong survived, so she was strong herself. She grew up in the South at a time when women, particularly Black women, didn't have many rights. But she was the opposite of a shrinking violet. She was known for her hair-trigger temper. The word was out in Sealy: you didn't mess with Red. I knew that better than anyone.

The way she grew up, violence and death were just a part of life.

Example one: When she was a little girl, about ten years old, her dad blew the top of a man's head off. The victim, whose name was Oliver Horse, had once been her dad's friend, but they got into a fight, and the guy beat him within an inch of his life with an agricultural weighing scale. My mom's dad was hospitalized, unable to move for months, and while lying in that bed, he made a vow: if he ever got out of that bed, he'd kill Oliver Horse.

It took more than a year, but he got out of that bed. One day, he got on his horse and buggy and went into town to get shotgun pellets so he could shoot some rabbits to eat. On the way back, he spotted his enemy on horseback. He loaded up his shotgun with the pellets and shot the guy dead. Telling the story, my mom would always say: *He shot Oliver Horse off a horse.*

In another time, in another place, he would have spent the rest of his life in prison. But in Wallis, Texas, in the 1910s, the government didn't care if one Black guy killed another. Instead, they cared about the land my mom's dad owned. The prosecutor let him skate, on the condition that he sign over his land to the government and get the hell out of town. That's how my mom wound up moving from Wallis to Sealy, about twelve miles to the north and west.

Example two: My mom's brother also killed someone. He was married to a woman who used to step out on him with a white police officer. My mom's brother was a heavy drinker just like his own dad was, so the cop would find him in the bars and lock him up on a public drunkenness charge, go sleep with his wife, then let him out the next morning. One day, while nursing a bad hangover, my mom's brother called his wife into the room and shot her dead.

Example three: My mom had been married before she met my dad. Her first husband, named Harold Jackson, was a drinker, a gambler, and an abuser—during one of the times he was hitting my mom she pulled a gun on him. At a certain point, she left Harold and took up with my dad, and one night, she and my dad went to a beer hall together. Harold was in the backroom playing cards with some guys, and at a certain point he came out with a big, boozy smile on his face. He'd won a lot of money in the game and was feeling good, so he grabbed my mom and started dancing with her, saying, *I wanna dance with my baby.*

But one of the guys from the back room had other ideas. He was sure Harold had been cheating in the card game. So right there, in front of everyone, he pulled out a gun and killed him.

So *that* was the world my mom came from. To her, being a good parent meant raising your kid to be tough. When I was about twelve, I came home crying one day because my cousin had beaten me up. My mom didn't hug me or say, *There, there.* No, she scolded me for crying and told me to get back out there to show I wasn't afraid of him. *Boy, you cannot be doing this. You cannot have people pushing you around,* she said.

At the same time, she knew how dangerous the world was, and she did her best to protect me. I was sheltered because she hardly let me out of her sight: kids from my neighborhood would play down the street on the dirt road I grew up on, but she wouldn't let me past the streetlight. When I'd complain and ask her why she wouldn't let me do this thing or that thing, she'd slap me in the mouth and say, *Because I said so.* And that was that.

I was careful in terms of getting involved with girls: my mom had seen too many kids who'd made babies with each other, ending their lives before they had really begun. I was a star athlete at a Texas high school, but I didn't lose my virginity until my senior year.

Drugs and alcohol were out of the question. Her dad, her brother, and her ex-husband were all drinkers, and so were lots of other guys around Sealy. She used to talk about Black people sleeping off their hangovers and say: *The white man is thinking while the Black man is sleeping. That's how they get ahead of you.* To her, being a drunk was playing into the white man's hands. She drank some wine here and there—Manischewitz was her drink of choice—and now, as an adult, I enjoy alcohol in moderation too. But I've only been drunk a handful of times in my life.

Breaking Viola Dickerson's rules was something you simply did not do, or even think of. You didn't *rebel* against her—that was out of the realm of possibility. Parents made the rules and kids followed them. That was it. I remember being in the grocery store with her and this white kid was talking back to his mom—*I hate you*, etcetera—and his mom was just *taking* it. My mom watched this with steam coming out her ears. I remember thinking she was gonna kick *my* ass.

My mom was by far the toughest out of all my friends' parents. My best friend, Gary Hill, was more daring than I was; he was smoking weed and having sex when he was twelve or thirteen. One time, he asked me to hold onto a joint for him. My mom would routinely search my room, so she found it. Then she went ballistic on me.

—*What the fuck is wrong with you!! I will* kiiiiilllll *your ass!*

I had to rat out Gary.

I was scared of my mom as a kid. I knew that she loved me, but I'd always wonder why I'd gotten this mean old lady for a mom. At the same time, I was inheriting her qualities. By the time I was in high school, I was exactly like her: fiercely proud, a hothead, a kid who got into fights at the littlest slight, one who wouldn't start fights but would never back down from them.

One time in biology class in my junior or senior year, this white kid I never liked called me Kunta Kinte, after the character in *Roots*, the TV series about slavery that was airing at the time.

—My name's not Kunta Kinte, I said.

—Kunta.

—Don't call me that again.

—Kunta.

I slapped him across his face. I was my mother's son.

The teacher told us to take it outside: it was forty-something years ago in Texas, so teachers would do these sorts of things. We started fighting, but right then, the principal, named Allen Harwell, walked by. We both got suspended: him for three days, me for five.

I thought about what my mom had told me after Little League try-outs: *It's just different for us.*

At the end of our suspensions, we were told we had to go back and get a couple of "licks" from Principal Harwell—a paddle on the ass. After that, they told us we had to shake the principal's hand.

That stirred something in my mom. She wasn't gonna have her Black son get whooped by a white man and then have me shake the man's hand. *She* could whoop my ass; a white man could not. So the day I went back, my mom came with me—and she brought her pistol with her.

She got in the principal's face, asking him why I got five days while the white boy got three. Harwell said it was because I'd cursed: I'd said the word *fuck*, and worse yet, I said it in front of a group of girls.

—Girls? Most of 'em have fucked anyway, my mom said.

Thankfully, cooler heads prevailed and the situation got defused. I wound up taking the licks but I didn't shake the principal's hand, and we all went on with our lives after that. That day, I was proud I had a mom like mine, raising me the way she was.

◆

All those qualities I got from my mom—my pride, my strong will, my unwillingness to be pushed around—are why I'm where I am today. But they've also gotten me in trouble and led me to act in ways I regret. As I've gotten older, I've learned to temper my mom's qualities with ones I got from my dad.

Kary Dickerson had salt-and-pepper hair, a deep, booming voice that he used sparingly, and the respect of everyone in Sealy. He laid track for the Southern Pacific Railroad and was a hard worker and a good provider. He was a good man, everything a man should be: kind, gentle, wise, and decent, a "speak softly but carry a big stick" guy whose words carried weight. He was very different from my mom, but the relationship worked because their personalities balanced each other out, and underneath their personalities they had similar values.

Around town, everyone, white and Black, addressed him as *Mr. Dickerson*. It always made me proud the way people looked at him. He had two kids from his previous marriage—my brothers Preston and Odell—and he was of no blood relation to me, but I never doubted his love for me. Any guy can make a baby, but that man was my *father*.

He was my rock, and *his* rock was his Christian faith. He read the Bible constantly and knew it backward and forward, but he wasn't one of those Bible thumpers who brags about how godly they are. Everything about him was understated, including the fact that he embodied what a Christian should be and what a man should be.

He was a deliberate, thoughtful guy. His main hobbies were gardening and carving things out of wood with a pocketknife. Both showed how patient he was. He was good with his hands and loved to work on cars. Whatever he was doing, I always wanted to be with him, to tag along with him.

He had that kind of calming personality: you just wanted to be around him because he always made you feel everything was gonna be okay. I used to love sitting outside with him for hours: I'd ask him to tell me stories from the Bible, or about the old Negro League ballplayers he'd seen play, like Satchel Paige.

He was much more into baseball than football—baseball suited his calm temperament—but he always supported me when I started getting into football. He had a saying, one of the many sayings he had that seem to get more true with each passing year: *Whatever you do, do with your might, 'cause things done by halves are never done right.*

He had a bunch of those sayings—*It takes a minute to get into trouble but a lifetime to get out*—because he was a man who lived by a code. My dad gave me a feeling of stability that a lot of kids growing up around me didn't have.

But he had a bad heart, basically all my life. Ever since I could remember, I kept having a recurring dream that he would die. Every time after waking up, I'd need a few moments to reassure myself that it was just a dream. I was always shaken up afterward.

My dad and I talked openly about his health and my fear he would die. There was a major open-heart surgery that he could've gotten because he had really good health insurance through his railroad job, but he thought it was too risky because of his age. He tried through his faith to reassure me that everything would be okay, whatever happened. He'd tell me that death was a part of life, that the body was just a shell, that I shouldn't cry for him or worry about him because he knew his soul was going to heaven.

—*Don't feel bad for me, because I know where I'm going,* he'd say.

But that didn't make me feel any better. The thought of losing him was literally my worst nightmare.

Then came November 3, 1977. I was seventeen, in class in my junior year of high school, when the announcement came on the loudspeaker: I was to report to the main office. If I didn't know it then, I knew it when I saw the looks on the faces of the administrators when I walked into the office.

He'd had a heart attack, like I always knew he would. When they found him dead in our house, he was lying down, with a calm expression on his face. His face rested on his hands, which were neatly pressed together. His fedora lay to the side of him. He was peaceful. He died like he lived.

But I was torn up. To this day, I get emotional when I think about it. It still feels like my time with him was cut short, that I was ripped off. I was a seventeen-year-old who needed his dad more than ever. At his funeral, at his casket, I collapsed to my knees and bawled. It was my first experience with grief.

The week he died, I had a football game against our rival, Bellville. My mom said my dad would've wanted me to keep doing what I loved to do, so I played in the game. But the news about my dad had gotten out, so before the game, the other team's fans mocked me by bringing out a casket.

A few weeks later, I had that recurring dream that he'd died. For a moment after waking up, I felt a huge sense of relief, as if the whole last few weeks had been a dream. But this time, it wasn't. The reality hit me hard, and still does.

◆

I am who I am because of my parents—who are not even my biological parents.

I always called my biological mom, who'd gone to live with Viola and Kary when she was a little girl, Helen. Helen got pregnant with me at fifteen in the back of a car; it was the first time she'd ever had sex. The father was a high school football star named Richard Seals. He had no interest in being a married father and he had some colleges looking at him, so he left Sealy for Houston and later got a scholarship to play running back at Prairie View A&M, a historically Black university in Texas. Much later, I heard he had the exact same running style I did: upright, smooth, gliding. I didn't meet him until I was seventeen.

Here's where it gets complicated: I grew up around Helen—but for most of my childhood I had no idea she was my mom or that I'd been adopted by Viola and Kary.

Helen lived right next door on our dirt road with her husband, and she and everyone else told me she was my *sister*, who just happened to be much older. In a way, it was sort of true: Viola had adopted Helen from *her* biological mom, my grandmother, when she was six or seven, and Helen called Viola "Mom," just like I did. Helen and I were really close, as a normal brother and sister are: I could talk to her about everything in a way you can't with your parents.

Of course I always had the question in my mind: *Why are my parents so much older than everybody else's?* But when you're a kid, whatever you're brought up around just seems normal. I really didn't think about it much.

Until one day in sixth grade.

I had a young teacher named Ms. Bonnie Ruth Holiday—I can't even remember what class it was but I remember that Ms. Holiday was young, about Helen's age, and had a crush on my biological dad's brother. Ms. Holiday and Helen had never gotten along. Helen was a very attractive woman, and someone had once told me Ms. Holiday had always been jealous of her.

That day, she told me to stay after class. When everyone else had cleared out, she asked me: *Have you ever seen your daddy?*

I was confused. I told her yeah, of course I had.

—*No, boy. Your* real *daddy. They haven't told you that?*

Then she told me the story. She did it out of spite for Helen. That was the first time I heard Richard Seals's name.

After school that day, I rode my bike home and asked Viola about it. She tried to deny it at first, but it wasn't long before all hell broke loose. She called Helen on the phone and I heard a lot of yelling and cursing. I heard Viola say she was gonna shoot Ms. Holiday. At the center of it all was me, but I had no idea how to react.

My dad pulled me aside. He was calm and reasonable as always, and he broke everything down for me in his levelheaded way. The way he made sense of it put me at ease about everything, and still does. He told me Helen was my real mom, and my real dad was out of the picture. But he loved me, Viola loved me, and Helen did too. And we were a family—just as we'd been before Ms. Holiday said what she'd said.

He said they hadn't told me because they didn't want to hurt me. That they thought it was best for me if I didn't know. I don't know what I think about their decision. What I *do* know is they made it with my best interests at heart, just like they did everything with my best interests at heart.

And that was basically it. People don't believe me when I say this, but I never really thought about it much after that. Everything reverted back to the way it was before Ms. Holiday said what she said. Nobody—Viola, Helen, Ms. Holiday, people in town—ever brought it up to me again. My dad's words stayed with me: the important thing was that I had parents and a family who loved me. A stable family. A together family—which wasn't the case with a lot of kids on the other side of the tracks in Sealy. I had everything to be thankful for, so I never saw this as some major childhood trauma, and still don't.

Helen and I would joke about it afterward. Sometimes, she'd scold me over one thing or another, and back before I knew the full story, I'd shoot back, *You ain't my mom!* After I found out, I'd say that whenever she got on my case, and we'd both laugh.

Years later, I got to know my biological father. You might say I forgive him—except I never felt I had anything to forgive him for. I was surrounded by so much love that I never felt abandoned by him or had any negative feelings toward him. He's a nice guy who I consider a casual friend. I call him Richard. He went on to have a few children he was close with. He owned a gas station in Houston and did well for himself. He was always cool with me, and he didn't do the thing a lot of biological dads of star players do, trying to get back into their son's life just as they're becoming a big football prospect.

Plus, I have sympathy for the fact that he wasn't ready to be a dad. Years later, when I was in my twenties, I fathered a child and didn't handle it well either. I practically didn't see my daughter for the first three years of her life. After that, I slowly came to my senses and grew up, and eventually became the dad I should've been all along. The point is: I know people can change and improve.

◆

I almost wasn't adopted by Viola. My grandmother wanted to adopt me, too, and she and Viola fought over me. You can call that the first Eric Dickerson recruiting war. Even though it didn't get the same publicity as the one years later when I was the top high school player in the country, it was far more important.

I was two or three years old and had been living with Viola because

Helen was living with her. But my grandmother Johnnie Mae loved boys, and she wanted to adopt me. She lived in Houston with her husband Horace, my grandfather, and they had three boys between them. Helen was their only girl, and, likely for that reason, she always treated her terribly, which is why Helen had gone to live with Viola and Kary. In my grandmother's mind, her boys could do no wrong and Helen could do no right.

So, when I came along, my grandma wanted another boy in the house. But Viola wasn't having it. She flat-out refused, and when Viola set her mind to something, she usually got her way. What clinched the argument for her was that my dad had really good insurance through his railroad job.

That's how Viola became my mom, and that's the reason you've heard of me today. My grandmother loved me, and I was very close with her, but had she raised me, there's no way I would've made anything of myself. She pampered her three boys, spoiled them rotten, and as a result they amounted to nothing.

All of them had problems with drugs, alcohol, or the law—sometimes all three. My uncle Joe was a drug addict who was always in and out of prison. Once, he cut a man's throat, but my grandma couldn't admit it to herself: *Joe didn't do that! Joe's a good boy*, she'd say.

Viola saw what was happening in that house and hated it. It was exactly what she prided herself on *not* being as a mom. *Those boys ain't worth shit*, she'd always say.

Getting adopted by my parents was one of those fork-in-the-road moments. I look at those uncles of mine and think about what could've been. *There, but for the grace of God, go I.*

Several years into my pro career, I remember my grandfather called me up on the phone. He was at the end of his rope with his sons.

—*Eric, I got a problem*, he said. *I got three grown-ass men living with me...*

The problem was they weren't grownups. Living with my grandma, who told them how great they were every second of the day, they never had to learn how to stand on their own two feet. I was lucky to have a mother like mine.

CHAPTER 2

FRIDAY NIGHT LIGHTS

I was scared to death before my first football game.

I was in seventh grade and I'd been dreaming about playing for years. But my mom was against it and wouldn't sign the papers to let me play. She thought the sport was too rough. She thought people weren't meant to bang into each other like that. She saw bad things down the road from it. She was right, as it turned out, but I wasn't thinking that way at the time.

I went to my godmother and had her sign those papers. My mom didn't like it but she eventually relented. She knew it was *that* important to me. It was Texas, and football was everything. I played baseball (I was a center fielder and a good lefty hitter) and basketball (I later played varsity in high school and could dunk from the free throw line before anyone knew who Michael Jordan was) but those sports didn't compare to football.

A Friday night football game in Sealy, Texas, made nowhere feel like somewhere. When I was younger, going to the game was the only time my mom let me out of her sight. Life in small-town Texas, on the other side of the tracks, is slow and limiting. There's endless space but no opportunity. The football game made you feel like you were a part of something: you'd smell the popcorn and the hot dogs, and see the cheerleaders. The floodlights would make the grass a bright shade of green. There was no place to sit; people were standing around the track. You couldn't find parking for blocks. The Sealy uniforms—black helmets, black pants, black jerseys with gold numbering like the Steelers—were *sleek*, and made our guys look cooler than the opposing players.

When I was little, I used to go watch practice: those football players were gods to me. I didn't know what I wanted to do when I became an adult. But I knew I wanted to be one of those guys.

And here I was. In seventh grade, playing for the school team. It wasn't quite the Friday night lights, but it was my first organized football game. I was wearing the pads, about to run and tackle for real. On the other sideline were the Waller Bulldogs, and they were hooting and hollering and looking tough and mean—and all of a sudden I wanted no part of it.

I wondered what I'd gotten myself into. This was before Rec Specs were invented, so I was wearing my prescription glasses. My legs felt like jelly. Fear took over my whole body. If someone would've given me the chance to undo the decision I made by signing up, I would've done it and walked away for good.

Then the opening kickoff came to me. And I ran it back for a touchdown. I remember the feeling of the wind in my face, the exhilaration of breaking away. It was incredible—I still haven't gotten over that feeling. Before that, I had no idea I was so much faster than everyone. I had no idea how good I was.

I ran for six touchdowns that day. I'd never had that much fun in my life. I had always loved football in my imagination, but now I loved it in my bones.

•

My middle school teams went undefeated in seventh and eighth grades. I was good, we were good, and we talked about the things we were gonna accomplish when we got up to the varsity level.

But the plan hit a roadblock: before my freshman year, we heard we were getting a new coach. Ralph Harris was his name, and he had a reputation. He was a white guy from East Texas, and back then, *East Texas* meant one thing: he didn't like Black kids.

Harris turned out as advertised. He was tall and wiry, severe in his presence, with a creepy, soft-spoken way of speaking that seemed sinister to me. He had about a hundred thousand rules—all of which seemed to exist for the sole purpose of punishing the Black kids: no Afros, no chains, no facial hair, and he'd find the most minute rules to enforce. Black kids made up about half the roster, but for some reason, *we* were always the ones running laps. It was always *us* that had the messy lockers or the uniform violations. It reminded me of what my mom always said: *It's just different for us.*

My freshman year came and went: I played flanker and wore number 88, but I hadn't really grown into my body yet. Sophomore year I was ready: I was the starting running back wearing number 19. But Coach Harris kept fucking with us, and things got worse and worse.

The way my mom raised me, Harris and I were on a collision course. I wasn't gonna take any shit from a white man. Once, I mouthed off to him, and a Black janitor overheard. The janitor got angry and scolded me: *How you gonna talk to that good white man like that?*

That pissed me off. *Good white man.* As if *good* and *white* were the same thing. That mentality was common in Sealy. We used to call them "Mister Charlie's Boys." A Mister Charlie's Boy was the type of Black man whose spirit has been crushed by the white man, so he aligns himself with him. The type of Black man who lives his life in fear and resents those who don't.

My teammates and I weren't like that. We stood up to Harris. And one day, in the middle of season, came the last straw: there was some dumbass rule that our shoes had to be on the very bottom of our locker, and that if they weren't flat on the locker floor, you got in trouble. That day in practice, Harris came in, made a fuss about our lockers, and then made us run the bleachers. We bitched and moaned about it, but we ran, like we always ran. For twenty or thirty minutes, all of us Black kids sweated our asses off. And then my cousin Bobby Byars decided he'd had enough.

—Man, I don't need this. I fucking quit. And he jogged into the locker room.

Bobby was one of the smartest guys in the school. He was a bookworm and a high achiever who worked summer jobs at an energy company in Houston. When my mom wanted me to study harder, she'd always say, *Why can't you be more like Bobby?*

That day, we all decided to be more like Bobby. One by one, we all jogged into the locker room. By the time it was over, all but one of the Black kids on the team had quit.

I loved football, but not as much as I hated my racist coach.

◆

All of a sudden, football was gone. Who knows what would've happened to me if I'd stayed away. Become one of those guys in Sealy on street corners, with their bottles in brown paper bags? I'd like to think I had more discipline than that, and that my mom would've kept me on the right path, but who knows?

A lot of the kids I grew up around didn't make much of themselves. My best friend Gary Hill, who ran a "faster" life than me and was drinking and having sex? It caught up to him pretty quickly. He got a football scholarship to the University of New Mexico, but he blew it when he got a girl pregnant. After that he was in and out of prison and basically drank himself to death. A bunch of guys I knew fell into alcohol or drug abuse. I'd see them back in town not many years later and they'd have no teeth.

Some people did better: some of the girls became schoolteachers. Bobby Byars is an engineer at that energy company where he worked summer jobs.

Here's the thing about being a poor, Black kid in America: for many of us, the most important decision we'll ever make comes when we're teenagers. Upper-middle-class white kids have plenty of chances to get it right. We only get one.

I owe my career to a local guy named James Abernathy. He was short and about as wide as he was tall, so everyone called him Shack. Despite his appearance, he was a well-known ladies' man who was married with a family in the nearby town of Brookshire but had one of his many girlfriends in Sealy. And he was really involved in the regional sports scene: he seemed to know every player and coach and be at all the games. He was popular, a shoot-the-shit-with-anyone guy, one of those guys who was always *around*.

One day, he pulled up to my house in his car and said he wanted to take a ride with me. I hopped in and we started driving around Sealy. Past the sleepy downtown. Past the dilapidated houses. Past the guys hanging out on the corners.

—*Let me ask you something*, he said. *What do you see?*

I didn't know what he meant. *I don't know . . . nothing?*

—*Exactly. Nothing. Because there's nothing in this town.*

He told me I was destined for bigger and better things—something I'd always felt since when I was a boy saying, *I'm the king*. He told me football was my ticket out. That if I didn't want to play for Coach Harris, he could pull some strings in Brookshire and have me play there. That quitting was a huge mistake, because he'd been following the sport a long time and I was hands down the best runner he'd ever seen.

That was news to me.

I thought of myself as a good football player, but one of the best in the area, spanning years and even decades? Hadn't crossed my mind.

I knew there were such things as college and pro football, but the thought of me personally getting a scholarship, or making big money in the pros? Also hadn't crossed my mind.

When you come from Sealy, your worldview is limited like that. But Shack opened my eyes, and the upshot was that I returned to the team my junior year and so did the other Black guys.

That was my one chance. Thanks to Shack, I didn't blow it.

◆

Things came together for me on the football field my junior year. I rushed for 2,000 yards. We went 8–2, though we missed the playoffs. Recruiting letters started coming: Texas schools, USC, Michigan. Shack had been right.

My friends and I didn't have to grovel to get back on the team. A few days after Shack took me on that ride, Harris came by my house. He said that he hadn't handled everything right, he wanted to wipe the slate clean, and he was asking me and the other Black guys to come back. I said I'd think about it.

I came back but we never saw eye to eye. From then on, we just kind of stayed out of each other's way. Whenever we were near the goal line, he'd call a QB sneak with our white quarterback rather than giving me the ball. This got on my nerves because when you scored a touchdown, you'd get your name in the paper. To this day, I'm convinced he was doing that just to fuck with me.

You'll hear a lot of athletes talk about what a positive influence their high school coach was, but that obviously wasn't the case with mine. Years later, after I'd made the NFL, Harris crossed paths with a friend of mine, who called me on the phone and then surprised me by putting Harris on. I remember hearing that quiet, creepy voice for the first time in decades. All of a sudden I got a chill down my spine and my heart started beating fast like I was sixteen years old, and I worried about what I might have done to get into trouble. For good and for bad, it's amazing how much power coaches and teachers hold over you when you're that age.

But Harris had called to apologize. He said he'd thought about everything through the years and realized he'd been wrong about how he'd treated us. I heard him out and accepted the apology. I appreciated the call, to an extent. I forgave, but I never forgot.

I never liked the man, but I learned to coexist with him. After I went back on the team, I'd learned playing for him was a means to an end, and that I was ticketed for things beyond him. I had become a major prospect—and what made everything click was that I'd found another gear of speed. I'd always been fast, but as my body filled out, I became even faster and more explosive.

I ran track in addition to football, and I really loved it: there's something about being fast that's exhilarating in a very simple way. But ever since I'd started running competitively in seventh grade, there had been a kid from Bellville named John Jackson who *always* beat me in the 100. Jackson had the opposite build from me: he was five foot seven and real muscular, with an explosive, compact stride. I was tall with a long stride, and when I was younger I was a little bit gangly. Every time we raced, he'd beat me. It became really frustrating because I'd look at his numbers in the paper, and I'd have better numbers! But when it was just me and him, he'd always win.

My dad knew I'd grow into my body a little bit more and become more explosive. *I know it's frustrating,* he'd tell me. *But I'm telling you, you'll outrun him one day soon.*

My dad died before he got the chance to see it. It was my junior year, after the football season, and Jackson and I squared off at the district meet. All my family members were in the stands and I was hyped.

I jumped the gun at first. Then Jackson jumped the gun. Then, because I was being careful, I got off to a slow start while Jackson got out fast. But I didn't panic, and I kept my smooth gait and ran him down. From that day forward, I never lost to him again.

That race was such a confidence-booster, and it helped me in football: I always felt smooth when I ran, and after that, I knew to trust my speed, and that I didn't have to muscle up. That my body was a machine and that the smoother the machine ran, the better.

Coaches had always been on my case about the way I ran: they said I ran *too high* and I should hunch over more. It was a knock I heard even after I got to the pros. Coach Tom Landry of the Cowboys told Rams coach John Robinson that the Rams had made a mistake by drafting me so high. Sometimes, because I ran so smoothly, coaches thought I wasn't trying hard enough. But winning that race against Jackson solidified that I'd been doing the right thing all along, and that I knew my body better than anyone. Coaches would keep saying those things, but after I beat Jackson, I ignored them completely.

•

Senior year was That Championship Season. The year everything went right. It's still the most cherished sports experience of my life.

We were a smaller school, competing at the 2A level in a state where the huge schools were 4A back then. (Now they go up to 6A.) But no matter the level, being state champions in Texas is a big deal, the type of thing a town like Sealy never forgets.

And our team was close-knit: I've played with some teams with good chemistry (the Rams years) and teams that were full of back-stabbers (the Colts), but that Sealy team set the standard for a group of guys who fought for each other. We all grew up together, so it was almost like we were a family. The team was about 50/50 between whites and Blacks, but it didn't matter. Everyone on that team was tight. We used to say that when you play for the Tigers, you're only one color, and we all believed it.

I was absolutely dominant that year. A man among boys, too big and too fast. All that season, it felt like there was no top speed I could reach, that I was doing something I was put on Earth to do. It's an amazing feeling: you've been given a talent by God and you're putting it to use. I don't say this arrogantly, because it really felt like *the gift* and *me* were two separate things, and I was just the vessel for it. It's almost a spiritual feeling.

We crushed everyone that year and rolled into the playoffs. But in the first playoff game against Splendora, things got dicey. We were playing at Tully Stadium in Houston on an Astroturf field, my first game ever on an artificial surface, and I sprained my ankle severely. The pain was bad and it didn't seem possible to put any weight on it. My friend Gary Hill filled in at running back and we won the game, but the ankle was in bad shape and I didn't think I'd be able to play the next week in the quarterfinals.

That game was against Hamshire-Fannett in Pasadena, and before the game, a trainer for one of the local schools—an old Black trainer, actually—said to me: *I'm gonna show you a trick.* Then he "spatted" my ankle, taping it outside the shoe to form a kind of boot as reinforcement. And it worked! I played and we won—and from that point on, I was a believer in spatting my ankle. One time in college, I got lazy and forgot—and wound up hurting the ankle. After that, I *always* did, and I never had any ankle problems again.

We won our next two playoff games in blowouts, setting up a trip to the championship game against Wylie, an all-white team in the Dallas suburbs. They were the defending state champions—and they had a reputation for being racist as hell. There was a big thing about where we'd play the game because we didn't want our players and fans traveling into hostile, racist territory. Finally, it was settled that we'd play the game at Baylor's stadium in Waco, a halfway point. We chartered thirteen buses to get our fans there. It was cold, with temperatures in the 30s, but our fans were ready and raucous. The town of Sealy had been waiting for this.

The Wylie kids—players and fans—were calling us the N-word from the moment we took the field. I'd dealt with a lot of racist shit in my day, but that was the first *and* last time I was ever called that by opposing players. And how did I react? I laughed. I can't explain why, but I thought it was funny. Maybe I laughed to cover up a deeper pain. Maybe I knew the Wylie guys were just a bunch of scared kids who knew they were gonna get their asses kicked. That's racism, right? It's just a bunch of insecurities projected outward.

That's exactly what happened. We had way too much speed for them. They actually scored on us first, but then I scored a touchdown on the ensuing series and we wound up blowing them out, 42–20. I rushed for 311 yards and 4 touchdowns.

The bus ride home is one of the best memories of my life. It was like a big, rolling party on the Texas highway, like we owned the whole state. Some kids from our school drove up alongside the bus and started passing beers to us. It felt good to be champions. It felt good to be young.

CHAPTER 3

THE TRANS AM

People used to joke that I got so much money at SMU that I took a pay cut to come to the NFL. That was me: Eric Dickerson, face of the SMU "scandal." As if the real face of the NCAA's corruption was a Black teenager from a dirt road in Texas. As if every school wasn't doing the exact same thing or worse.

I'm gonna tell you what SMU gave me, and about the Trans Am—or the "Trans A&M," as people joke. But first, I have to call bullshit on the whole thing. On the NCAA, which is nothing but a cartel that exploits the free labor of young, mostly Black kids. On these so-called scandals, which made me and other players out to be some sort of criminals. It's all bullshit. As I wrote earlier, the real scandal wasn't how *much* I got paid. It was how *little*.

The NCAA, man. What a bunch of pimps. Think about it: like pimps, they make money on the backs of people who feel they have no other choice. Like pimps, they keep their employees in line by scaring them.

It's wage theft. College athletes are the backbone of a billion-dollar industry. Clemson head coach Dabo Swinney makes more than $9 million a year. ABC, CBS, and Fox paid a combined $1.5 billion for the rights to televise college football in 2020. The guys playing the games supposedly get a "free education"—but good luck with that when you're working a more-than-full-time job for a football corporation and know they can yank your scholarship if you don't perform, and when you come from a poor area with underfunded schools and therefore aren't prepared academically.

That's college football: young, Black men do physical labor for free while old white men make the money. Sound familiar?

◆

I wasn't aware of any of this my senior year of high school, before all the recruiting craziness started. When your mom doesn't let you past the streetlight for most of your childhood, you're sheltered and know very little about how the world works. Later in high school I started getting out more—I used to visit my grandparents and cousin in Houston— but I was still a naive, small-town kid. I'd only been out of the state of Texas once, when I went to Oregon on the train through my dad's job.

Then it all began. I was the top recruit in the country over guys named Elway and Marino, and suddenly the coaches started coming, lining up behind each other. Guys I'd seen on TV, suddenly at my house as if I were living a fairy tale: Barry Switzer, John Robinson, Fred Akers.

It was fun at first. People *wanting* you. Seeing your name in the paper and on TV. Putting Sealy on the map for something other than the mattress company.

But the attention got old quickly. The phone ringing off the hook, recruiters pulling up beside me when I got off school and showing up to restaurants, harassing my friends and relatives. Sometimes boosters, sometimes assistant coaches, most of them white, all of them invading my space and saying the exact same things: *You're the second coming. We need you; you're gonna play right away. Don't go to that other school; they don't treat their athletes right.*

My mom put it in perspective for me. *Boy, those white men don't care about you. They care about what you can do for them. The white man is the biggest user there is.*

One time, I was sound asleep in the middle of the night when my mom knocked on my bedroom door. It was about 1 or 2 a.m. She told me there was a white man on the porch who wanted to talk to me.

It was an assistant coach from A&M. He had a crazed, desperate look in his eye, like he was almost crying. He asked me if I was considering A&M. He said, *If I don't get you, I'm gonna lose my job.*

I had no idea how to react. Then he asked again: *So what are you thinking?*

The only thing I was thinking about was sleep. I mumbled something and went back to bed.

Had I just dreamt that? Was I dreaming this whole thing?

Meanwhile, I felt a lot of jealousy from people in town—and the disappointing thing was that it came from the Black community. Nobody said anything to my face, but I'd hear from relatives and friends that so-and-so person was talking shit: *Why are they recruiting him? He can't play at the college level! So-and-so is better than him!* The strange part was, the white people in Sealy were totally behind me; it was only the Black people who had a problem.

That's something a lot of successful Black people have to deal with: haters, who hate you because you're gonna make it out and they're not. They've lived their whole lives with limited horizons. By reaching beyond Sealy, you're showing them just how small their world is.

It's the same mentality of that janitor I talked about: the guy who scolded me for mouthing off to Coach Harris, who in his mind was a *good white man.* That janitor was a guy who was trapped in his mentality. He had been gotten to by the white man. He resented that I hadn't.

During this whole period, I really missed my dad. It was a time in my life where I really needed a male figure. More than that, I needed his calming presence, the way he could make sense of everything and make me believe that everything was gonna be okay. After he died, my mom softened a bit, as if she was trying to fill his role. But there was only one Dad. I missed him more than ever.

Many kids have their high school coach to guide them through recruiting, but Harris was no help at all. He was leaning on me hard to go to the University of Texas; I suspect he had some side deal worked out with them where they'd give him a coaching job. *Your State School—*

that's how he'd always put it when he told me I should go there. As if I owed the state of Texas something. At a certain point I told him point-blank: *I don't need you, and if recruiters wanted to get at me, they could talk to my mom and my grandma.*

After that, Harris started bad-mouthing me, telling the coaches that I didn't take school seriously and that I'd be a problem academically. Wherever I went for college, at least I'd be getting away from that man.

◆

Of course there were benefits to being the top recruit in the country. Like the Trans Am—the one I drove to school my senior year, a week before national signing day in 1979. I was eighteen then and now I'm sixty-one, and it's *still* the thing people ask me about the most.

For all these years, I've been telling people my grandma bought it for me. That's the truth—technically. But yeah, there's a lot more to it than that.

To understand the story, you first need to understand the pressure I was under to go to A&M. Sealy's in East Texas, about seventy miles from College Station, so it was an A&M town. The town's biggest businessman, Clarence Shear, who owned the livestock feed store, was a big A&M booster who had given me a job the summer before. And the man I called my stepdad—my biological mom's husband—had a side deal with A&M, where they offered him a house in Westview, the white part of Sealy, and a few head of cattle. (Cattle were big in Texas recruiting in those days; recruiters promised to keep your freezers stocked with meat.)

But I wasn't into A&M. First, I didn't like their uniforms. That was a big factor for me as an eighteen-year-old who wanted to look cool. Second, the student body was about two-thirds male. When I visited, it seemed like there were no girls, just a bunch of dudes from the school's Corps of Cadets in military uniforms. They didn't even have cheerleaders; they had male "yell leaders." It just wasn't what I was envisioning for my college experience.

So that was the backdrop. But then came the moment when a different A&M recruiter came to my house and, in front of my mom, opened a suitcase containing $50,000. I never saw the suitcase, but my mom came over from the next room and told me what happened.

—*Eric, that's the most money I've ever seen in my life.*

My mom was still cleaning houses at the time. She got some money from my dad's railroad pension as his widow, but I'd looked at her checking account a little bit before that and saw $20 or $30.

Then she said: *But if you don't want to go to that school, do not take these peoples' money.*

That was my mom. Yes, she was tough, but she always put me first. And I didn't like that school. And, believe it or not, I didn't take that money.

What if I had blown out my knee? That $50,000 could have bought a big house in Sealy.

It's a fair question, but that thought didn't cross my mind. A lot of things didn't cross my mind back then—including the fact that someone could make millions of dollars playing pro football. You have to understand how sheltered and naive I was. That's true of most kids being recruited to play college football. That's why the NCAA's system of exploitation works.

Even though I turned that money down, A&M stayed after me and remained in the picture—there was *that* much pressure for me to go there. And then, a few weeks later, I mentioned to my stepdad in passing that I really liked the new Pontiac Trans Am. I'd seen it at a dealership on I-10 that I used to drive by to visit my grandparents in Houston, and I just *liked* it: the bird on the hood, the fins on the side, how sleek it was.

It was an innocent comment. Under normal circumstances, I wouldn't have remembered even saying it. But recruiting isn't a normal circumstance, and before I knew it, I was talking to Shear, the big A&M booster in town.

—*We can make that happen*, he said.

Then he told me to go to the dealership, and all of a sudden I'm there with my mom and my grandma, then the staff is telling me to *pick any car on the lot.* That's the way things were in those days: one minute I'm a broke kid idly fantasizing about a nice car. The next, a bunch of grown-ass men are falling over themselves to give me that car.

I had my pick of a Corvette and three Trans Ams: black, silver, and gold. I liked the gold one.

The dealership guy said he'd be right back, that he just had to make a phone call. When he returned, he gave my grandma the paperwork to fill out.

Now, until the present day, I've always said publicly that my grandparents bought me that car. My grandfather made good money from his job as a crane operator at a steel mill, and my grandma's name is on the paperwork, so that's technically true. But behind the scenes, A&M had agreed to reimburse her. And that, my friends, is how the notorious Trans Am was paid for.

I didn't know any of this at the time, however. I learned it a few years later, when I was already in the pros and I asked my mom. But at the time, I wasn't trying to look a gift horse in the mouth, and I didn't need to know everything. The only thing I knew was that I was driving home the finest car, by far, of any kid in Sealy, white or Black. I'll never forget peeling out of the lot and feeling the engine underneath me. The new car smell, the vinyl dashboard, and the 8-track player I was gonna play my Commodores and Isley Brothers on. I was *excited*, and my mom and grandma were excited because I was excited. I couldn't wait to go to school the next day.

Of course when I showed up at school, it became huge news—across the state, across the country. A couple days later, my cousin and I pulled up to a restaurant and got out of the car, and a photographer snapped a picture of us and the car that wound up in the *Houston Post* the next day.

Not long after that, an A&M booster or an assistant coach (I can't remember) asked me to commit to going to A&M. With all the media coverage of the car, and with all the excitement around town about the car and what that potentially meant about me going there, I said yes.

It was a verbal commitment. I was eighteen and it seemed like the thing to say to make a lot of adults happy. But my heart was never really into it, and I'd soon renege on it. I know a lot of A&M fans are still pissed at me about that, but I *really* don't care: if they want to be pissed at a kid whose head was spinning and was being pressured by all different kinds of adults, then that's their problem and not mine.

There's this urban legend that angry A&M boosters destroyed the car, but I'm here to tell you that never happened. I had the Trans Am my first few years at SMU, before I sold it to my best friend and fellow SMU running back, Charles Drayton. Thanks to an SMU booster named George Owen, I was driving a Corvette by then.

So that's the truth, the whole truth, and nothing but, straight from the horse's mouth. Is that such a scandal? That the best player for one of the best teams in the country got a nice car? I don't think so. I think I deserved that car—and a lot more than that.

◆

Of course, immediately after I got the car, I became an object of suspicion. That always happens when a Black person in America is seen driving a nice car, or wearing a nice suit or watch, or moving into a nice neighborhood. If we have these nice things, it means something's fishy, and we're the suspects.

I was sitting in class one day when someone knocked on the classroom door. The teacher answered and I heard someone say "Eric Dickerson." Then the teacher called me out of class. It was an investigator from the NCAA, there to talk about the Trans Am.

He was a Black guy, and his demeanor was calm but official enough to scare the shit out of me. To me, the NCAA was the law: we all had heard those horror stories of kids messing up their scholarships by accepting gifts. The kids were publicly shamed, looked at with disdain and probably a little glee for pissing away their opportunity. In nearly every case, these kids were Black. I didn't want to be one of those kids.

When the NCAA guy asked about the Trans Am, I told him, *You have to talk to my mom and grandma.* I might as well have said, *Get me a lawyer.*

That was the beginning of the NCAA's investigation. The guy stuck around for about a month, poking into the finances of my mom and grandma like he was the IRS or the FBI. He'd interview people around town, then drive to Houston to interview people about my grandma. At one point, he told my grandma the NCAA had received a thousand phone calls about that car, or about seventy to a hundred a day. To this day, I don't know who was calling, but my guess it was people connected to schools other than A&M, and maybe also jealous people around town who resented all the attention I was getting.

The whole time, I was nervous. My grandma tried to reassure me. *That car was bought legally, under my name. They're not gonna find nothing on it,* she'd say. But I was sure it was only a matter of time before they busted me.

Finally, the investigation ended, and we were in the clear. It was a huge relief—but it was also thrilling. I knew there were tons of people, both locally and across the country, who were hoping the NCAA would turn up something. They wanted to see another Black kid get busted and have his future ruined. Well, fuck *all* those people. I still had my promising future. And my Trans Am.

♦

Everyone still talks about the Trans Am because it was such a big thing at the time, and it gets brought up when people talk about all the SMU stuff. I get that, but for me, a lot of what stands out about my recruiting experience took place *before* the Trans Am.

Like the first time I went to L.A. for my USC trip, and was surrounded at the airport by a bunch of people with shaved heads, wearing robes, chanting, *Hare Krishna, Hare Krishna, Krishna Krishna, Hare Hare.*

That was 1979 L.A. for you. I had no idea what was going on until USC running backs coach John Jackson rescued me.

—*Don't worry about them. They're the Hare Krishnas.*

He whisked me away and a little bit later I was at USC practice, where I spotted O. J. Simpson across the field. I'd grown up idolizing him because he was a tall running back, like me. When I first started playing, being tall practically disqualified you from playing the position, and he changed that perception.

I walked up to him and introduced myself, and told him I wanted to break his record. He thought it was funny and said, *Well okay, young man. Good luck!*

But I wasn't into USC. As much as I came to love L.A., it seemed too far away and too different when I was eighteen. I crossed it off the list.

Texas was another school that I never considered seriously. *Your State School.* That's what Harris called UT, and that's what the white assistant coach who came to recruit me called it. I forget his name but I'll never forget his arrogance. He knew SMU was recruiting me so he told me, *SMU will never beat us. Ever.*

He knew USC was recruiting me, so he told me it was too far away. He knew Oklahoma was recruiting me, so he told me Barry Switzer was sleeping with his secretary and his assistant coaches' wives.

Then he put it to me this way: *If you don't come to Your State School, we'll make sure that when you get out of college, you'll never get a job in the state of Texas.*

I couldn't believe my ears. But looking back, I shouldn't have been so surprised. Behind the ass-kissing of recruiting is contempt. At the end of the day, the white coaches know they have the power and the Black kids don't.

But I wasn't gonna take that. I'm Viola Dickerson's son. You challenge me, I'll come right back at you. I looked that coach dead in the eye and said, *Man, fuck you.*

Then I went to the other room to get my mom: *Mama, make him leave.*
—*What'd he say?*
—*That white man told me that if I didn't consider My State School, he'd make sure I'd never get a job in Texas.*

—*Oh, hell no! You'll never go to school there!*

I came to learn that same coach used that tactic on other recruits. Texas was off the list too.

◆

Oklahoma was my top choice the whole time: they wanted me, I wanted them. To me, Oklahoma represented everything that college football was supposed to be. It was far enough from home but not too far. I'd watched the Sooners in the Orange Bowl every year, it seemed. I loved the way the horsedrawn wagon came onto the field before the game, and I loved their uniforms with the OU on the helmet. I loved Billy Sims, the running back who went on to win the Heisman Trophy and become the first pick of the draft, and the cool way his towel hung down from his uniform, a style tip I took from him. I liked Barry Switzer, how enthusiastic and flamboyant he was. Switzer showed up at my high school championship game wearing a mink coat.

Switzer came over and showed us the tapes of Oklahoma playing in the Orange Bowl. He created an aura about the program, and I was enthralled. He told me they took care of their players—and that he could help my family.

I told him: *I'm committed. I wanna come.*

But my mom wasn't having it. She insisted I stay in Texas. The whole time Switzer was playing his tapes and doing his spiel, my mom stayed silent, which I knew was a bad sign. Sure enough, once everyone said their goodbyes and left, my mom turned to me and told me I wasn't going to school there.

I was crushed.

—*Mama!*

—*Nope.*

—*Mama!!*

—*Eric, that man is a liar. And I don't trust him.*

My mom had never been on an airplane before and Norman, Oklahoma, was a six-and-a-half-hour drive. The distance, I think, was the deal-breaker, and Switzer never stood a chance from the beginning. Because of that, all of his smoothness and swagger, which I loved, rubbed my mom the wrong way.

I had to beg her to let me go on my Oklahoma recruiting trip, and when I came back, I wanted to go there even more. It was *college* like I'd always pictured it, the culmination of everything I'd worked for. We got picked up at the airport by people in OU gear; the band came out and played for all the recruits; I met Billy Sims; the town of Norman had a vibe to it that just said *football*. I even met a girl there, the daughter of a professor, a Lebanese girl named Mary, who I went back to see several times after that. She was smart and worldly. Everything about Oklahoma seemed first-class to me.

But my mom didn't budge. Number-one recruit in the country or not, in Viola Dickerson's house she was still the adult and I was the kid. I was angry with her, and I thought if my dad were still alive, I could get her to see things my way. But he wasn't, and that was that.

Looking back, I think the fact that my mom nixed Oklahoma opened the door for A&M. I figured that if I wasn't gonna go to my top choice, I might as well make my stepdad, Shear, and a lot of people in Sealy happy.

But here's the thing: my mom was tough, but she cared deeply about my happiness and she could read me like a book. And in the days after I committed to A&M, she sensed I wasn't happy.

We were at a barbecue at my biological mom's house, and I was playing cards with my stepdad and some other guys when my mom and grandma called me over. They asked if I was happy with my decision. I said no.

I brought up Oklahoma again, but it was obvious again that was going nowhere. Then both of them started talking about Ron Meyer.

◆

The best way I can describe Ron Meyer was that he was a white man who was comfortable in Black peoples' houses. The first time he came to visit my biological mom's house, he yelled out, *Y'all cooking up some catfish?* We sat at the table with him and he enjoyed every bite.

I liked him immediately—and regardless of my problems with college sports, I'll always love that man, who died in 2017.

He brought an instant, infectious energy. The first thing I saw on him was his Super Bowl ring from the Dallas Cowboys' 1971 season (he'd been a scout) and his gold, diamond-encrusted Concord watch that looked like a bracelet. Everything about the man was sharp, clean. His clothes. His hair. His crackling speech. His sense of humor.

The man was a salesman, straight up. He could give you a bag of rattlesnakes and tell you to reach your hand in because something good was inside, and you'd do it. (What he was selling at SMU wasn't much better: his team had won sixteen games total in the three years he'd been the head coach.) He wasn't a standout tactician—his thing was hiring great X's and O's guys under him—but he was the best motivator I've ever been around. If I heard one of his speeches right now, I'd be ready to run out of the tunnel and play a football game.

He worked my mom, called her up on the phone over and over, charmed her the way he charmed everyone. He made a promise to her and that's what I think clinched it. *If I ever have a problem with him,* he told her. *I'll call you. Because I know you can handle it.*

I liked him a lot and I liked SMU, but I wasn't sold. As the top recruit in the country, I had a hard time picturing myself at a school that didn't have a winning tradition and seemed small-time.

But I was intrigued. I liked that they were building something by going hard after the Dallas and Houston areas. There were a bunch of guys I'd seen in the papers over the previous couple of years: Michael Carter. Charles Waggoner. Harvey Armstrong. Michael Charles. Craig James.

I liked that SMU was in Dallas. In the era when the TV show *Dallas* was blowing up, it was a city on the make, a place where *things were happening.* Meyer always emphasized that: to him, other schools—from Baylor in Waco, to Texas in Austin—were *country.* During my recruiting trip to SMU, they brought me and other recruits to Texas Stadium, where we'd play our home games, and we looked at the blue seats and the opening in the ceiling and the shadows on the field, and we went the locker room where Tony Dorsett, Danny White, Drew Pearson, and Too Tall Jones put on their pads. I wasn't a Cowboys fan—in fact I hated them growing up—but it was a rush. They lined us all up on the 20-yard line and flashed our names on the scoreboard: *SMU Welcomes Eric Dickerson.*

All that, and I liked the uniforms too.

Harvey Armstrong took me around on my recruiting trip. A year older than me, he was a defensive tackle from Houston who'd go on to play eight seasons in the pros, during part of which he was my teammate and friend on the Colts. He took me to some clubs and tried to sell me on the school. *We're young and we're good,* he said. *This is a team that can win a national championship.*

My mom and grandma were big on SMU, and they acted fast after I told them I wasn't happy with A&M. They called up a local SMU booster named Robin Buddecke and told him I was still potentially interested in SMU.

The very next morning, Meyer chartered a flight to Rosenberg Airport, about ten miles from Sealy, and we all met up at Buddecke's house, which was nearby. One of the keys to Meyer's success at SMU was that he had access to charter flights and hopscotched the state of Texas on planes, basically out-hustling other coaches for recruits. That's exactly how he got me.

Meyer asked me: *Eric, would you like to come to SMU?*

A big part of me did, though a big part of me still had reservations. But I was worn down by the whole recruiting circus and wanted it to end. My mom and grandma wanted SMU. I wanted to please them, and at least I wouldn't be going to A&M.

—*Yeah, I'll come.*

I signed the letter of intent, the only thing I ever signed during the whole process despite previously committing verbally to both Oklahoma and A&M. Finally, it was over.

But I wasn't all-in on SMU. Something about it still seemed second-rate to me. I always kept an eye on Oklahoma—to this day I root for them when they're on TV—and that fall, when I saw the incoming freshmen at OU, it made me mad because I knew they weren't as good as me.

To make myself feel better, to convince myself I made the right decision, I'd go back to something my mom told me when she was trying to sell me on SMU over Oklahoma. She told me Oklahoma already had a history and it would be hard for me to distinguish myself, and that at best I'd be one more in a long line of great players. *Go to SMU,* she said, *and you can make your own history.*

She was certainly right about that.

So now for the big question: How much money did SMU pay me to get me to come?

The answer is nothing—at least not initially. That fall, after I showed up to campus, I started getting $1,000 a month, which I'd get my whole time at the school, per an agreement my mom and grandma had worked out. (I'd go into Ron Meyer's office and pick up an envelope.) So I got my envelope, and in addition to that, George Owen, the SMU booster who was a Dallas real estate guy, bought me a Corvette and gave me some money for clothes, meals, and other things here and there.

But that was it. All that talk about me taking a pay cut to come to the NFL couldn't be further from the truth. For the amount of revenue I produced for that school, I got chump change in return.

And about the SMU "scandal?" Well, SMU wasn't close to being the worst offender. SMU didn't come with a suitcase full of $50,000 like A&M did—and I know for a fact that guys who went to Texas, Houston, Oklahoma, and A&M got a lot more than even that, and *then* got a lot more than I got throughout college.

No, SMU got scapegoated. We got picked on because we crashed the party of the blue bloods by getting really good when we weren't supposed to. We were an upstart that challenged the establishment powers, so the rules were selectively enforced against us—a tradition as American as apple pie.

CHAPTER 4

THE GREAT WHITE HOPE VS. THE BLACK BUST

The very picture of "culture shock" was me during my freshman year at SMU.

Go to any college campus and you'll find mostly upper-class kids. But SMU is a school for the super-rich. Sons and daughters of oil barons. Dallas society kids who wore preppy clothes, drove BMWs, and had second homes on ranches in the Hill Country.

I'd never seen so many white people in one place. They were there because their parents could afford it. They walked around campus with the carefree demeanor of people who'd *inherited* the place just like they'd inherited everything else. Meanwhile, I was there because of the money I was making for the school, as basically an employee. I felt out of place, like an imposter, as if someone was gonna tap me on the shoulder at any time and tell me the jig was up.

For a kid who'd grown up in the Black part of town, with dirt roads and dilapidated shacks, I can't tell you how strange it was to be plopped down on a manicured campus with white faces as far as the eye could see. If you saw a Black person at SMU in 1979, it was a good bet he was my teammate or some other athlete.

Talking to girls was intimidating. They came from rich families and had tales of debutante balls. I had no idea what to say to them.

All of it was a lot to handle. I was homesick and unhappy. And my freshman year football season was turning into a disaster.

There are no two ways about it: coming from a small, 2A school, I simply wasn't ready for the physical punishment of college football. Weight training wasn't stressed at my high school and my body hadn't filled out; I was still long and lean. But I was going up against guys who'd been in weight programs for years. I was still built like a boy, but I was going up against men.

I played well in our opening win against Rice, rushing for 120-something yards and 2 touchdowns, but then the injuries started piling up: A bad concussion against TCU in the second game. Then my hamstrings started bothering me. Then I hurt my ankle when I forgot to spat it. Then my thigh. Then my shoulder.

I spent most of that season in struggle mode, nursing this or that injury, never really acclimating to the speed and physicality of the college game. I rushed for just 477 yards total and the team went 5–6. It wasn't what anyone was hoping for when I committed to SMU as the top recruit in the country.

Meanwhile, Craig James, another running back who'd been recruited along with me to SMU from the Houston area, took the job and ran with it, rushing for 761 yards. Craig was an example of a kid from a big, suburban school with access to a first-class weight room and coaching. He was strong, polished, and ready to play from the start. I wasn't any of those things.

The media had a field day with the contrast, playing Craig and me off against each other. I was the top recruit in the country and I was getting outplayed by the underdog white kid. It played into all their prejudices. Craig was the blue-collar, all-American boy; I was the fast Black kid who was always injured. To the media and the alumni who were pulling for him, he was the Great White Hope, and I became the villain, the Black Bust.

I was shocked and hurt by how vicious the writers were. They wrote column after column saying I was a *bust*. Saying they should *take my scholarship away*. There was real anger in those columns, as if I'd done something to hurt them personally. These were grown-ass men, some of them with kids around my age, and I could never understand why they were being so . . . *mean*. Would they have treated their own kids that way?

Of course they wouldn't have. But that's the thing: white America doesn't see Black nineteen-year-old boys as kids. It goes back to what my mom always used to say: *It's just different for us.*

From that point on, I never trusted the media and always kept them at arm's distance. Once bitten, twice shy. Let the other guys be the media darlings. Let them be the guys who charm the writers and make them laugh. That would never be me.

Craig and I would split carries my whole time at SMU, basically a 50/50 split until senior year. (There was another Texas running back in our class, Charles Waggoner, who was lightning-quick and was actually better than both of us. But he hurt his neck midway through freshman year and never played again.) I later came to realize that sharing time with Craig was actually a blessing in disguise because it saved my body for the pros. But I hated it at the time.

As much as the media tried to pit us against each other, though, Craig and I were always cool. I never held anything against him and I consider him a lifelong friend. He's a straight shooter, a *what you see is what you get* kind of guy. I didn't like the situation but I've always liked Craig.

We hit it off before even getting to SMU: I'd heard of him because he was the star of Houston Stratford, a powerhouse school that won the 4A title, the highest level back then, and he called me on the phone once he heard I was coming to SMU. He brought up the Trans Am and he cracked me up by asking if we were gonna be on probation. We talked about being excited to come to SMU and said we were gonna start something memorable.

It was a prophetic conversation, but my freshman season was one to forget.

◆

Schoolwork was a struggle, too, another aspect of college I wasn't ready for. Freshman year my grades were terrible, and I had to go to summer school afterward to stay eligible. In high school, I was an average student, but the work in college was way harder. As with everything else, I felt that my small-town background had left me unprepared.

I don't know how it is with college football players nowadays, but in those days, we were expected to do our work. We had tutors, but they didn't do your work for you, and the professors didn't grease you through to stay eligible. I wound up getting up to speed academically, but I never graduated.

Coming to the big city of Dallas was another challenge I wasn't ready for. Everything seemed fast. Everyone on campus and in town seemed to know the angles—except me. I felt like a country boy, a rube.

One time, I went to get my Trans Am cleaned at the car wash, and there was a guy there playing three-card monte with some other guys. I watched, and at a certain point, the dealer said he'd bet me $5 I couldn't find the card.

I bet $20, the last $20 in my pocket. I lost it. Then I bet my watch, and lost that.

Then I saw the guys who'd been playing before ride off in a car with the dealer. That's how I knew I got got.

•

All of my struggles, with everything, left me feeling frustrated. I became the typical angry young man, struggling to find his place in the world. I found myself getting into fights.

One time, I was walking back from practice after injuring my thigh, basically feeling sorry for myself. When I passed by the swimming pool, three older guys on the team—Lott McIlhenny, Eddie O'Brien, and Norm Rivers—jumped me and threw me into the pool, fully clothed. I thrashed around, panicking. I didn't know how to swim.

When I got out, I lost my shit. I ran back to my dorm room where I had a big Bowie knife; I grabbed it and ran back to the pool, where the guys were still hanging out. As I approached them, I started yelling, "I'm gonna kill you motherfuckers!" I was Viola Dickerson's son. Nobody was gonna embarrass me like that and get away with it.

A bunch of white girls saw me and screamed: a big Black guy with a Bowie knife—that was their worst nightmare. Lott and Eddie jumped into the pool, but I wasn't gonna follow them in, so I turned toward Norm and punched him in his eye, cutting it open. Our team strength coach happened to walk by and broke up the fight before things got really out of hand.

Another time, we were in study hall and I was bored and cutting up. The study hall teacher was named Dr. Barr—everyone called him Doc Barr—and when he left the room for a minute, I wrote on the chalkboard "Doc Barr sucks," just for some laughs.

There was an offensive lineman who I'd never gotten along with, this redneck-type guy from Colorado named Mark, and after I wrote that, Mark said to me, *Eric, you're so immature*.

I wasn't gonna take that, so I shot back, *Man, fuck you*, and we took it outside the classroom.

A bunch of the guys surrounded us. Mark said something to me, so I slapped him across the face. He was completely shocked, and when I saw the look on his face, I slapped him again.

Then he took a big swing at me and missed. I popped him in the eye and got him in a chokehold. It took about four guys to get me off him before we went back inside the classroom.

The funny thing was that Mark and I later became cool. A few months later, he invited me over to his house for some smoked fish he'd caught back in Colorado. But at the time, I wasn't cool with him just like I wasn't cool with a lot of things.

◆

Things got better my sophomore year. We went 8-4. I stayed healthy and rushed for 928 yards, splitting time with Craig, who rushed for 896. I acclimated to life on campus and I wasn't nearly as homesick. All those things Ron Meyer and guys like Harvey Armstrong had said when they recruited me were turning out to be true: we *were* building something special. We had talented, young players and a bright future.

But sharing the running back job with Craig wasn't sitting right with me. (Our offensive coordinator, Steve Endicott, made that decision, not Ron Meyer.) I had shed the "bust" label from the year before. I had gotten used to the contact and speed of the college level. I was confident that my ability was second to none and I was ready to become a star, but I was only a part-time player. One of the reasons I'd gone to SMU was that my mom had convinced me that I could create my own legacy, but that wasn't gonna happen if I was on the bench half the time.

I don't say this to be boastful, but when you're a great athlete, you *need* the chance to show it. It's like being an artist: it's how we express ourselves, and if we can't do it, it feels like something is festering inside.

The frustration built up in me. Finally, I was sitting in my dorm room with Charles Drayton, our fullback and my best friend to this day, and I told him: *Man, I need to get outta here.*

As for where I'd go, there was never any doubt: Oklahoma. The school I'd been smitten with ever since Barry Switzer showed up at my house and showed me the tapes of the Sooners in the Orange Bowl.

I decided to take matters into my own hands and to call Switzer myself. I looked up Oklahoma's athletic department and called it, and then I asked for the football office. A woman picked up the phone.

—*Can I speak to Barry Switzer?*

The woman on the other end said she was Suzy, Switzer's secretary. She asked who was calling.

And then I froze. I just didn't say anything, and after a few seconds, I hung up.

Not long after that, I went home. I told my mom I wanted to transfer. She shook her head and then took out a piece of paper—and drew a line down the middle. On one side was SMU. On the other was Oklahoma.

She made a list of things I was guaranteed to have at SMU that I wasn't guaranteed at Oklahoma: I had a guaranteed scholarship at

SMU—but if I transferred to Oklahoma, I'd have to sit out a year, and anything could happen. Although I wasn't playing at SMU as much as I'd have liked, I was still playing, and there was no guarantee of that at Oklahoma. On and on she went, and by the time she was done, the piece of paper had all checkmarks on the SMU side and none on the Oklahoma side.

Then Viola wrapped it all up.

—*I'm an old woman. I'm not going to Oklahoma. It gets cold there. Take your ass back to SMU.*

So I did.

CHAPTER 5

THE PONY EXPRESS

I met my best friend in the world, Charles Drayton, my freshman year at SMU. We were next to each other on the stretching lines. He was a sophomore running back from Florida hoping to climb the depth chart and start one day. I was one of several guys they brought in who would make that impossible. He had every reason to dislike me. But he's too good-natured a guy. We clicked immediately.

I had a million questions that first year, and Drayton answered every one of them, from the playbook to classes to girls to everything else. He helped me time and again, over and over again, even though he didn't have to. I clung to him. *I couldn't have gotten rid of you if I tried*, he always tells me.

He's a funny guy, and a loyal guy. He's the godfather to my children, just as I am to his. I introduced him to his wife. I couldn't ask for a better friend.

The foundation of our relationship is total honesty: we're like brothers who don't hold anything back. When I was screwing around on my college girlfriend Monique, he called me out: *Dick, man, don't do her like that—she's a good girl.*

When I couldn't stand my oldest daughter's mom, to the point where it was getting in the way of my relationship with my daughter, he called me out: *You have to get along with her for your daughter. You might not like it, but it's better for you and your daughter in the long run.*

It's not healthy to hold on to all that hatred.

When he was buried on the depth chart at SMU, still trying to make it as a running back, I told him he had no shot, and suggested he move to fullback, where he'd primarily be a blocker and not a runner. He did, and then became the starting fullback for our famous Pony Express backfield, the indispensable guy who did the dirty work that made the express run.

After sophomore year, I felt more comfortable in the offense after having some success. But Drayton told me I still had work to do, that I had to get bigger and stronger to fulfill my potential. He put it to me bluntly: *Dick, man, if you're as good as they say you are, you can do your thing even if you're not getting enough carries.*

Those words inspired me. I'd never been a weightlifter. Up until that point, I'd gotten by on my speed, and the only weight training I did was some machines here and there. But Drayton stayed on me and taught me how to lift, just like he'd taught me everything else about being a college player, like how to block. He didn't have close to my natural talent, but he had a tremendous work ethic and was a student of the game. Being around him all the time helped my career immeasurably—and it started to pay dividends junior year.

My body was different when I stepped on the field that year. I was filled out. My first two years, I was a fast boy trying to run away from the men on the other side. Junior year, I was running with power. That speed and power combination would become my defining trait, and it all started in the weight room with Drayton.

My production skyrocketed: I rushed for 1,428 yards, for 5.6 yards a carry as a junior. I still split carries with Craig, but by then it was becoming obvious that I was ahead in the pecking order. Drayton told me a story about one game that year, when he was standing on the sideline with Lott McIlhenny, another running back and a very close friend of Craig's. It was a close game, and I was starting to get going, and Lott said to Drayton, *If they wanna win, they better leave 19 in the game.*

They did, and we did.

•

Junior year is when we put it all together as a team. We went 10–1, with our only loss a 9–7 defeat at home against Texas. Two years prior, we were doormats. Junior year we won the Southwest Conference (SWC). We had a slightly better record my senior year, going undefeated with just one tie, but junior year was the more talented team.

The Ron Meyer rebuild happened just like he'd promised: During his first three years, from '76 to '79, SMU won sixteen games. In '80 and '81, my sophomore and junior years, we won eighteen games. In the episode about our team for *30 for 30*, a series of sports-focused documentaries, Ron, while talking about recruiting me, said, *He bought the dream that I sold*. That was true. And in '81, that dream became a reality.

It felt good to take the league by storm and flip the script on those arrogant, traditional powerhouses. The SWC wasn't ready for our speed and option attack. Playing in Texas Stadium, we felt like a pro team: opponents would be in awe of the stadium, and the Cowboys players would watch us play. Our athletic director, Russ Potts, came up with the "Pony Express" marketing slogan. All of a sudden, we were a phenomenon.

Our team was a bunch of renegades. We might have played at the rich, white school in Highland Park, but we were mostly Black kids from either the deep country or the hood. *Hungry* kids.

And teams always underestimated us. We played Grambling at home our junior year, and I was up for that game. Grambling had recruited me and I liked a lot of things about the school and the program: the Black pride, the cheerleaders, the band and drumline, the legendary coach, Eddie Robinson.

I'll never forget the looks on their faces when we came out of the tunnel and they saw us. They'd assumed we were a bunch of white boys. Well, that was true for our school, but not us, and the Grambling guys were completely shocked. We whooped them, 59–27. I ran for a 62-yard touchdown, and hugged one of their cheerleaders.

We started getting recognized out in the Oak Cliff section of Dallas, where the Black clubs we'd go to were. Thanks to my booster, George Owen, I had a little money in my pocket and a Corvette to drive around. But it wasn't like I was living it up, and I wasn't getting paid a fraction of what I was earning for that school. Put it this way: I had a lot less money to spend than most of the kids who weren't on scholarship.

But I had a really good relationship with George—or Mr. O, as I called him. He'd give me that $1,000 every month, and I'd immediately send half back home to my mom. However unfair college sports are, I don't blame guys like Mr. O. The way I see it, a lot of those boosters were just trying to make things a little more fair. Different guys had different boosters—Craig's booster was Sherwood Blount—but only the top players were getting money. Drayton, for as valuable as he was to the team and me, didn't have a booster.

Mr. O was a good, funny, unpretentious guy who'd made his money in real estate and became a mentor to me. I'd met him on my recruiting trip when we went out to dinner at Campisi's restaurant, and we clicked immediately. He wasn't one of those stereotypical outlandish, braggadocious Texans, and I appreciated his understated manner. But Mr. O didn't last much longer: a few years later, as part of the NCAA sanctions against SMU, he got banned from associating with the school.

SMU was in the crosshairs of the NCAA going back to my sophomore year. I can pinpoint the moment it all began.

It was in the middle of the season and we were unranked, coming off two close losses against Baylor and Houston, when we went down to Austin to play Texas. They'd beaten us badly the year before. I hated them—I'd hated them from the moment that coach came to my house and threatened to bar me from getting a job in the state unless I committed there. I still hate them: I hate their uniforms, I hate their fight song, I hate that stupid cow mascot. A lot of us at SMU did, and that day, we ran the option down their throats and whooped them, 20–6.

After the game, all these old SMU alumni came to the locker room. Some had walkers, some had wheelchairs, and they were all emotional, saying they'd been waiting decades for this day. SMU hadn't beaten Texas in fourteen years, and never had defeated them on such a big stage.

Soon after that, the NCAA started interviewing guys on our team. I'm convinced it was Texas who dropped a dime on us. We were under the radar—but then we whooped their asses in Austin. After that, the law was after us.

They found twenty-nine recruiting violations; I guarantee you they could've found at least that many at any other SWC school. Our punishment was being barred from bowl games and television appearances during my junior year.

We took out our frustrations on the field. We knew we couldn't represent the SWC in the Cotton Bowl, but we won the conference anyway, which seemed like a good way to say, *Fuck you*. Our last game of the season was against Arkansas, and we called it the "Polyester Bowl" and treated it like our bowl game. We wanted to let everyone know that we were the class of the conference and that that year's Cotton Bowl—where Texas would beat Alabama—was second-rate.

The NCAA wasn't done with SMU, obviously. I remember meeting the player who brought the whole program down. By then I was in the pros, but I'd come back to Dallas to see people and sometimes go to dinner with Mr. O and the recruits. We were at Campisi's—where I'd been recruited a few years before—and from the start I got a bad vibe from one of the recruits, David Stanley. All dinner long, he kept telling me, *You're not that big . . . I think I could take you*.

He was joking, but he was trying to push my buttons, and was using me to prove something about himself. I was an All-Pro running back. I didn't appreciate it.

When we got up to leave the restaurant, I said to Mr. O: *This is a bad kid. Don't recruit him. He's gonna mess up stuff around here*. I wish he would've listened to me.

Then I got next to Stanley and grabbed his arm and pulled him tight to me: *Boy, you're a high school kid. Don't ever be talking to me like that. I will bust your ass up*.

Sometimes, I regret not doing it.

•

Ron Meyer left SMU after our junior season, when the New England Patriots hired him to be their head coach. Ron had always told us he'd never leave us for another college team, but the pros were a different story. I was happy for him but crushed for myself and our team.

We all loved Ron. The man had such a positive energy, which ran through the whole program. He believed in himself and SMU before there was anything to believe in. We were proud of what we'd built. My mom had been right: it was a lot more meaningful to make our own name at SMU than it was to carry on a tradition.

Our new coach was Bobby Collins, who'd been the coach at Southern Mississippi. He was brought in because our athletic director, Bob Hitch, was also a Southern Miss guy, and from the beginning, a lot of us knew Bobby and his staff weren't the right guys for the job.

Ron had Vegas swag. Bobby was a nice guy, but we all felt he represented a step down. Ron always told us, *I recruit guys to play on Sunday, not Saturday*, and he treated us like pros. Bobby treated us like high school players: he'd make us run full-contact drills in practice where we'd hit the shit out of each other. I was pretty vocal about that and got into it with the coaching staff. I told them, *We'll show up to hit on Saturday*. I thought we'd earned that, but the coaches didn't want to hear it.

The guys didn't like it. *These hillbillies are in over their heads*, we'd tell each other, and we were right: Bobby took over a program at its peak and basically ran it into the ground within a few years. Over his first three years, with the talent Ron had brought in and the reputation the program had developed, SMU went 31–4–1. His last three years, the team went 12–10. Then the NCAA imposed the "death penalty" on SMU—a one-year ban from competition—and the program hasn't been the same since. A lot of us felt the death penalty wouldn't have happened if Ron had stayed, and that they got caught under Bobby's leadership because those guys were amateur hour. Still, Bobby got a golden parachute of $850,000 afterward. All the while, the sports media were freaking out about some kids getting a few thousand dollars and some cars.

The difference between Ron and Bobby can be summed up in Bobby's most famous decision, made in our game against Arkansas.

We had an 11–0 record going into the game, the last of the regular season. With about three minutes left, down seven points, we scored a touchdown to pull within one point.

It was up to Bobby: Should we tie the game with an extra point, or go for two and the win? Bobby opted to kick the extra point and the game ended in a tie, which cost us the chance at a national championship.

We still were conference champions and still made the Cotton Bowl against Dan Marino's Pitt team. We won the game 7–3 and I was the game's MVP. Bobby defended his Arkansas decision by saying his two goals were defending our SWC title and going to the Cotton Bowl, and that the tie allowed us to accomplish both.

But that shit was weak. Ron would've never pulled that. Ron's whole thing with us was that our program was second to none. He wasn't someone who settled, and neither were we.

And who won the national championship? Penn State, and we finished second—even though they'd been blown out by Alabama mid-season and we didn't have any losses. We thought we were much better than them; we felt they were too slow. But the writers gave it to Joe Paterno because they loved him so much. They saw him as a harmless, cuddly grandpa and they saw us as a bunch of bad guys. Shows how much they knew.

◆

Missing out on that national championship was a bitter pill to swallow, because that senior year squad was truly *my* team. I was still splitting carries with Craig—it was about 55/45 in my favor by then—but I rushed for 1,617 yards and 17 touchdowns, averaging 7 yards a carry. After spending the beginning of my career feeling like a kid playing with grownups, I was a man among boys my senior year. I owed a lot of it to the work in the weight room I did with Drayton. I never forgot what he'd told me: *If you're as good as they say you are, you can do your thing even if you're only playing half the time.*

I had *so* much fun that year. It's an amazing feeling: doing what I loved to do at such a high level. Back then, my love for the sport was so pure, it was enough for me. I didn't think about the economics of college football, or the racial dynamics, or the exploitation. When I'd go back to Sealy, the guys on street corners smoking weed and drinking would give me a hard time: *Man, you the white man's slave!* But I didn't think about any of that. I was so happy to be doing what I was doing, and so grateful I wasn't one of those guys.

(One reason I was happy was my girlfriend, Monique Lawyer, a great person who I'm still friends with. I wasn't ready to settle down at that point, but Monique was a gem, and still is. It was a case of meeting the right person but at the wrong time.)

I finished third in the Heisman voting that year: Herschel Walker won it and John Elway finished second. I have nothing against Herschel, but that was ridiculous: He had 135 yards more than I did, but with 103 more carries. He averaged 5.2 yards per carry; I averaged 7. There was really no comparison, but Herschel had been a Heisman finalist his whole career and was a media darling, and I'd never been either of those things. Plus, Herschel benefited from a three-year hype campaign from his school, and my school didn't push me at all.

That's the part that still bothers me: if SMU had given me the playing time I deserved and marketed me, there's no question I'd have won the Heisman. In fact, I ran into Barry Switzer about ten years ago. He told me that had I come to Oklahoma, he would've made sure I won the Heisman. *There'da been no Pony Express,* he told me. *You'da been the Lone Ranger.*

Because I was a finalist, I got to go to the Heisman ceremony in New York, which was my first time there. And I hated it. It was dirty and crowded, with too much concrete and no trees. The people were completely different from how they were in Texas: in Texas, the custom is that you say hi, then the other person says hi back. In New York, if you say hi, they look at you like you said something about their mama.

I had a lot of really eye-opening experiences after that season, where I got out to see the world a little bit. I went to Orlando for Bob Hope's presentation of the Associated Press All-American team. But somehow, someone lost the bag that had my SMU uniform. At the last minute, they had to run to a sporting goods store to get me some plain white pants, a generic blue jersey with the number 19, and a plain white helmet for me to put under my arm when I ran out on stage. It was embarrassing: looking good is important to me, and I looked like a fool.

Then there was the Hula Bowl, in Hawaii. That week, I became friends with Dan Marino, Roger Craig, and Jamie Williams, who would have a nice long career as an NFL tight end. We were having dinner one night, sitting on a patio overlooking the Pacific, when I saw, for the first time in my life, the sun going down over the ocean. It was so slow, and so beautiful. Growing up in Texas, I'd never seen anything like it before. I decided I wanted to come back to Hawaii any chance I got, and that meant making the Pro Bowl when I got to the pros.

Right after that, I flew to Japan to play in the Japan Bowl, another all-star game. It was fun, but I was *way* outside my comfort zone. Nobody spoke any English. I remember being in the hotel lobby and a bunch of Japanese guys surrounded me, going crazy, saying, *Dickerson, number one player!* They'd bow—and I'd bow back. I went to a sushi bar with them later and I couldn't believe they were eating that raw stuff. I was disgusted, and I ate McDonald's the whole time I was in Japan. Now, after being in L.A. for almost forty years, I love sushi.

After the season was over, I knew I'd be a top draft pick. Mr. O connected me with an agent, and I stopped going to class and spent my time getting ready for the combine, the annual showcase for NFL prospects, which was in Seattle back then. I was a semester and a half away from graduating and my mom wanted me to stay in school, but things were moving too fast and I felt I needed to focus on preparing for the pros. I had it in my mind that I'd go back but I never did, and I regret that.

I stayed in my condo off the 635 loop and worked out a lot on my own. I knew how to train for running because of my background in track; I knew how to lift weights because Drayton had taught me. I didn't run a 40 at the combine, but I ran a 4.30 and a 4.34 on grass at a pro day, where prospects get scouted at their school.

At the time, a new professional league, the USFL, was ascendant, and I flirted with the idea of playing in it. But I talked to my mom and she shut that down:

—*Eric, who's been around longer?*

—*The NFL.*

—*You go to the NFL then.*

Once again, I'm glad I listened to my mom.

I knew the Rams were interested in me. That was the place I wanted to be. I liked the idea of being in L.A. I felt like I didn't get my just due at SMU, especially with the Heisman situation, so I was looking forward to being on the big stage. When I was a senior in high school and USC was recruiting me, L.A. seemed too far away. But four years later, after everything I'd experienced, I was ready. Plus, I loved the uniforms.

The Houston Oilers had the second pick in the draft, but John Robinson and the Rams traded up with them to take me in a deal that also involved the Seahawks. I was relieved: the Oilers were on a steep decline after peaking a few years earlier, and Earl Campbell was still there, so I didn't want to be in the shadow of another great Texas running back. Besides that, I'd spent the first twenty-two years of my life in Texas and it was time to see the rest of the world.

I was going to L.A.

CHAPTER 6

HOW VIOLA DICKERSON SAVED MY CAREER

You can take the kid out of the small town, but you can't take the small town out of the kid. And when you come from a place like Sealy, you always have the sense that people aren't paying attention to you, that you're being overlooked. A lot of athletes come from forgotten places, whether they're small towns or inner cities, and have that same chip on their shoulders. Mine got bigger after I didn't win the Heisman my senior year.

I knew the type of talent I had. I knew people didn't get to see it in college when I played for a program that wasn't one of the blue bloods and split carries with Craig.

But now I was the number two pick in the nation. Now I was going to L.A. Eric Dickerson, from a dirt road on the other side of the tracks, was going off to Hollywood to become a star. I thought about all those jealous old guys back in Sealy who'd always doubted me and said I wasn't that good. I thought about those miserable writers covering SMU who got off on calling me a bust. They could all watch me on Sundays.

After I got drafted in April, I flew into LAX and got picked up by a guy named Ray San Jose. I'd come to know him as a beloved Rams employee who did every odd job for the organization and was called

"Heeza," as in "He's a Ram." I was excited to be in L.A. and I saw that shimmering downtown skyline. But then I noticed we were driving away from it—and it was getting smaller and smaller.

I asked him: *Isn't that L.A. behind us?*

Yep, he goes, *But we're going to Orange County. The Rams are in Anaheim.*

I made a mental note. I'd never heard of Orange County before, but I'd come to realize there was a big difference between the O.C. and L.A.

We drove and drove, far away from anything that looked like a city, until we finally pulled into the team facility—which was actually a middle school. The meeting room was a classroom with those little flip-top desks. The changing room was in another building altogether. And the showers were really short because they were built for twelve-year-olds. I did another double take: *This* was the pros? Team facilities back then were nothing like today's, but even by the standards of the time, this was shabby. Our facility at SMU was ten times nicer than this. I made another mental note.

We went into a classroom, where some of the coaches were there to meet me. Then the owner, Georgia Frontiere, came in with John Robinson, who was in his first year with the Rams after a successful run at USC.

John had a big smile on his face and a friendly, backslapping demeanor. I hadn't seen him since my senior year of high school, when he tried to recruit me to USC.

I finally got you! was the first thing he said, and we both laughed.

I sized up right away that John had a similar personality to Ron Meyer and that we'd get along. He'd built a winner at USC by relying on the running game with great backs like Marcus Allen and Charles White. Now he'd come to the Rams and traded up for me so he could do the same thing in the pros.

The press conference was a little later, and it was overwhelming. I was happy to be in L.A. so my talent could have a big stage, but I knew navigating the media would be challenging. I've always been sort of shy, and I've always resisted being prodded by the media to say whatever braggadocious thing they'd prompt me to say. They do that with Black athletes especially: they make caricatures out of them, and a lot of guys go along with it because it's important to them to have the media like them. But I was secure in myself and didn't need the writers to like me. During that first press conference, the writers asked me if I thought of myself as the Rams' *savior*, but I wasn't going there. *I'm just here to play football* was all I gave them, and I felt their disappointment. It was a sign of things to come. The media and I would never see eye to eye.

After my press conference, I flew back to Dallas and met some people at Confetti's nightclub to celebrate. I'm not a big drinker. I like to have a drink or two to relax, but I can count on one hand the number of times in my life I've actually been drunk. I don't like the feeling of losing control, and I've never liked the way people behave when they're drunk—sloppy, saying dumb things—so I've never wanted to appear that way. But that night, I threw caution to the wind. Fuck it, I was the number two pick in the draft, going to L.A. I got as drunk as I've ever been.

◆

Training camp wasn't for another few months. Before that started, my contract would have to be worked out. Nowadays, there's not that much wiggle room when it comes to contracts of draft picks. There's a framework, and all the negotiation is at the margins of that. Back then that wasn't the case—which is how, after holding out for a couple of days, I wound up signing a horrible contract that was the seed of everything that ultimately went wrong between me and Rams management.

Four years and about $2 million, which included a $900,000 bonus—$600,000 of which, I later learned, was actually a forgivable *loan* that the Rams decided *not* to forgive after they traded me in 1987. During the most productive stretch any running back has ever had, I was one of the lowest-paid starters at my position for a part of it, and then in the middle of the pack for another part. It was a terrible contract even by the standards of the time. My agent, Jack Mills, was a nice guy, but he was in way over his head negotiating with the Rams, and when I learned how bad my contract was I had to fire him. My story is one of many in pro sports where a young, poor kid with no background in finance gets taken advantage of. Many of us are Black, and we're basically at the mercy of the old white guys negotiating our contracts.

I'll get into this more later, but the fact that I was giving the Rams my production at a fraction of its value makes the perception of me as *greedy* completely absurd. I've always felt that my reputation stems from two things: my days in at SMU, where they were supposedly paying me so much, and my bad blood with the Rams. In both cases, that view is completely backwards. In both cases, I generated huge sums of money and wasn't *close* to being compensated for my value. This isn't a boast; it's a fact. And yet *I'm* supposed to be the bad guy? That makes no fucking sense.

But we live in a country where Black people who are outspoken about demanding fairness are by and large painted in a negative light. When things went south with the Rams a few years later, the writers pounced: I became *Eric the Ingrate*. I became a *locker room lawyer*. It reminds me of what my mom always used to say: *It's just different for us.* The narrative about me had been set in motion, and whenever I bristled against it, it would only confirm that I was an asshole with a bad attitude. Would the narrative have been different from the beginning if I were white? There's no doubt in my mind.

But all this was years away. At the time, my contract was the most money I'd ever seen. I wasn't aware you could make that much for playing football, or anything close to that. I was happy and ready to go.

◆

Then came training camp. It was miserable. And because rookies had two weeks of camp before the vets showed up, it seemed like it was never gonna end.

I'd never liked training camp on any level. The fun part of football is *playing*, not practicing, and the difference between the two is the biggest out of any sport. But that first pro camp, at Cal State Fullerton, was shitty in a way I'd never experienced before, and it pushed me to my breaking point.

Ever since I ran for six touchdowns in my first organized game in seventh grade, football had always been *fun* for me, a *game*. But from early on in camp, it was obvious pro football was a *business*. You'd get up at 6:30 and from that moment on, you're going: breakfast, meetings, practice, lunch, more meetings, practice, more meetings, and finally curfew at 11:00. Pads and full-contact for both of those practices, and when you had any downtime, you were expected to study your playbook in your dorm room.

There were tons of guys—fifteen running backs, thirty receivers— and even though I was the second pick in the draft and a Heisman finalist with a big contract, I was so naive that it felt like I was competing with all of those guys for a roster spot. That added to the stress. So did the fact that I was on my own for the first time, 1,500 miles from home, and didn't know a single person.

Ten days in, I woke up too sore to move. Anyone who has ever played football on any level knows this feeling: *How the fuck am I gonna get out of bed, let alone put on my pads, let alone get beat up in practice?* I managed to get myself to practice but something in me had snapped. I'd had it, and during stretching, I told wide receiver Otis Grant, who I'd made friends with, that he wouldn't see me at evening practice: *Man, I'm outta here. This shit is crazy.*

It sounds insane in retrospect: I'd worked my whole life to get to this point and was about to just *walk away*. But that's where I was at, mentally. The best analogy I can think of was that it was like being interrogated by cops trying to get a false confession: you're so exhausted and at the end of your rope that all you can think about is going home, even if it means screwing yourself. The money didn't occur to me. What I'd do with the rest of my life after going back to Sealy didn't either. I just needed to get out of there.

After that practice I called my mom and told her I was coming home: *Mom, this is too much . . .*

That woman hated football. She hated the violence and the inhumanity of it. But what she hated more was the idea that her son was a quitter. She wasn't having it.

—*Boy, you ain't quitting! You gonna keep your ass there and stay with it!*

I didn't have an answer to her response. You don't talk back to Viola Dickerson. One, she's fierce. Two, she's always right. That woman saved me from myself too many times to count. That day, she saved my football career.

That evening at practice, I saw Otis.

—*I thought you were gonna quit?*

—*My mom wouldn't let me.*

He just laughed at me.

◆

All during rookie camp, the coaches would say that when the vets showed up, it'll be *different.* The speed would be faster, the contact would be more intense.

They were right. When the vets came, shit got real.

On one of the first days, we were doing a live pass-blocking drill. I was standing a few yards behind the action, watching Jackie Slater square off against Gary Jeter, the two of them just *going at it.* They were so big, and so ferocious, it was like watching two grizzly bears trying to kill each other: *Braw-waw-waw-waw-waw!!* This was the big leagues, no doubt. I was standing with Otis, and after seeing that, pass-blocking a guy like Gary was the last thing I wanted to do: *Oh hell no,* I told Otis. *This shit's too fast for me.*

A couple plays later they threw me into the drill. The defense did some pre-snap movement that confused me, and the linebacker I was supposed to block flew by me—I almost didn't see him—and got to quarterback Vince Ferragamo in an instant, tapping him on the shoulder instead of tackling him because it was training camp. It was the type of missed assignment that gets your quarterback killed in the regular season.

A coach barked at me: *Eric, who'd you have? Who's your man?*

I had no idea.

—*Rookie, get outta there before you get someone hurt.*

Another "welcome to the league" moment was when I first went into that locker room with those guys. I swear, that first day, it blew my mind. During the rookie minicamp it hadn't quite occurred to me that I was playing pro ball. But then—*boom*—right in front of me is Jack Youngblood, the guy who played with a broken leg in the Super Bowl and could've been John Wayne as far as I was concerned. There was Jackie Slater, who was already a wise old pro, and who'd go on to play thirteen more years in the league. There was Kent Hill, an offensive lineman who was sculpted like a Greek god, without an ounce of fat on his body. Nolan Cromwell. Jim Youngblood—who wasn't related to Jack. LeRoy Irvin. Guys with reputations that preceded them. I felt like I was ten years old, like I was the kid and they were all my dads.

My senior year of college I felt like a man playing among boys. Those first few weeks of camp it was the exact opposite. I was a deer in the headlights. Lost. The low point came during our first scrimmage against the Cowboys, who trained in nearby Thousand Oaks, when I got so nervous I forgot my assignments on every play. In the huddle, whenever Vince would call the play, my mind went completely blank, and I had to ask him what I was supposed to be doing. It was the most unsettling thing. It had never happened to me before and it never happened again.

Finally, they took me out of the game and my running backs coach, Bruce Snyder, started quizzing me on the plays. Slowly, my brain warmed up, and when I regained my senses, I went back into the game and actually played really well.

That scrimmage gave me some confidence, and in the next few weeks I started to feel more like myself. I started off third on the depth chart but soon enough I was the starter. The veterans began to seem more like my teammates and less like distant dads. If there was any resentment from them initially about how much money I was making, I never felt it. Those guys were cool with me. They knew I was there to work and win, and they respected that. I learned then that our locker room was filled with winners, even though the team had struggled the previous two seasons. I'd walked into a lucky situation: we were a close-knit team, where jealousy and ego took a backseat. I didn't realize quite how lucky I was until after I left the Rams years later.

Then, after a preseason game against Washington, when we saw the one-back offense they were using with two tight ends, John Robinson abruptly changed the offense from split backs to a one-back set—with *me* as the centerpiece. Being in the one-back was more comfortable for me. In the split-back formation, we were in three-point stances, but in the one-back, I was standing up, lined up 6 to 8 yards deep, where I was able to use my height to see everything in front of me and my speed to get a running start.

John was always a straight shooter, and the way he'd talk to me always gave me confidence. He told me: *We're gonna change the whole offense, and build it around you. You're the guy.*

That had happened abruptly: one minute I was a third-stringer who couldn't remember the plays, the next I was the guy an NFL franchise was building its offense around. I had worked my ass off for weeks and, thanks to my mom, pushed past a psychological breaking point. And here I was.

Just before the regular season, on an off-day, I went to Venice Beach with Otis Grant and Doug Reed, another rookie I'd made friends with. Since the start of camp, we'd been hunkered down in the dorms at Cal State Fullerton and had hardly gotten out. But finally, after all that misery and all that work, we took Doug's old Dodge Dart to Venice, three pro athletes in L.A.

There was the ocean. There was the boardwalk. There were the beautiful women, everywhere, of every color.

And then I saw it: a canary yellow Rolls Royce. It had that '80s California license plate, with the sun in the middle on top and the rays stretching out to the sides. Instead of a plate number, there was a word: "MAGIC."

He was six foot nine and holding court, with that huge smile on his face as always. A crowd formed around him, and got bigger and bigger. He was chatting them all up, the smile lighting up his face and those of everyone around him.

Magnetic is the word for that. Doug, Otis and I felt ourselves drawn in. We joined the crowd, waited our turn, and approached him.

—*How you doing, Mr. Johnson? I'm Eric Dickerson.*

He was cool immediately. *I know who you are. You're the first-round pick.*

We started talking, and I noticed just how big the crowd around us was. I'd never seen someone be so *adored*. Magic was exactly as advertised: a guy who made everyone's day and seemed to never get tired of it. At that moment, I realized that L.A. can make you a star on a level I never knew existed.

The regular season was starting in a few days. I was excited. I was ready.

Or so I thought.

CHAPTER 7

ROOKIE OF THE YEAR

Week 1. We flew into New York to play the Giants.

The day before the game, I went with a bunch of vets—Jackie Slater, LeRoy Irvin, Jack Youngblood—to the Museum of Natural History to see the dinosaurs. Two months before, I'd been in Sealy, in my childhood bedroom in my mom's shotgun shack. And now here I was. My rookie season was filled with surreal moments like this. I could never quite believe where life had taken me.

Some of those moments were cool, like seeing the dinosaurs. Some were scary. Like during practice before the week of our first game when running backs coach Bruce Snyder told me we'd put in a new play where the tight ends would run shallow crossing routes and I'd have to block the outside linebacker.

—*Ok cool. Who's the outside linebacker?*

—*Lawrence Taylor.*

That first game in Giants Stadium was at 1 p.m., with a bright sun that made all the colors—the green Astroturf, the yellow of our helmets, the Giants' blue—so vivid it was almost like it wasn't real. And Lawrence Taylor was screaming and cursing at us all game like a maniac.

He barked at everyone, nonstop. His stamina was impressive; L. T. was a different breed. *Motherfuckers* this and that, *Y'all ain't shit,* etcetera. He barked at me: *Motherfucker! You ain't gonna get no hundred yards!*

I just looked straight ahead and tried to avoid eye contact. I thought he was a certifiable crazy person.

Finally in the third quarter, the call came in for that play Snyder had talked about, where I had to block L. T. I lined up and he lined up, and I saw him in that stance, the most intimidating stance any defensive player ever had: standing up, leaning slightly on his front foot, his arms dangling, his body ready to explode with violence. Snyder had told me that I didn't have to stop his rush completely, I just had to cut his legs to get his hands down so our quick-hitting routes could develop.

At the snap, he rushed and I went down to cut his legs. I cut him good, and he hit the turf.

I don't remember if the play was successful. All I remember was that L. T. sprung up, grabbed me by my shoulder pads, put his face-mask right into mine and looked at me with the craziest, most intense eyes I'd ever seen before. *Hey bitch, don't you fucking cut me! You fucking understand me, punk? I'll fucking kill you.*

When people say, "I'll kill you," you assume it's a figure of speech. When Lawrence Taylor says it, you assume he means it literally. I was so scared the only thing I could think to say was, *Okay.*

And then I just left the field, straight to the sideline. And my coaches were like: *Eric?! Get back in there!*

—*Nuh uh. That man said he was gonna kill me.*

The coaches had no idea what to say to that. They told me to take a few plays off.

I went back several plays later. We won the game and I played okay but not great, with 91 yards on 31 carries, with my rookie nerves coming and going the whole time. After the game, I saw L. T. on the field and apologized for cutting him.

He screamed at me again: *Don't you ever cut me like that, mother-fucker,* and I stammered and apologized again. But then he went, *Man, I'm just joking with you.*

I came to know him after that and consider him a good friend. But I still think he's crazy.

My first NFL game was under my belt. If they were all that eventful, I didn't know how I was gonna to get through sixteen games.

•

My first few games turned into a struggle. The speed of the game was a lot to adjust to. After four years of college football, all my instincts were calibrated to the speed of *that* level, so that in the pros, with things moving so fast, I felt a beat or two behind. All sports are about timing, and when you're not used to the speed of the game, your timing's off and everything feels out of sync. Those first few weeks, I was holding my own but not playing especially well.

I invited Charles Drayton, my best friend from SMU, out to California to live with me that year in an apartment I got in Costa Mesa. He was standing on the sidelines for one of my first games and said his mind was blown by how fast everything moved. That says a lot: Drayton was a starter on an elite Division I team, playing with multiple guys who made the NFL. It goes to show how huge the leap is from one level to the next.

The violence of the pro game was kicked up a notch too. Unlike in college, these guys played *through* the whistle, which is another way of saying that even after the whistle stops blowing, they're still twisting your ankles and clawing at the ball. Early on, I developed a problem I'd never had before: I started fumbling. Six times in the first three games, to be precise. As a running back, fumbling the football is the biggest blow to your confidence imaginable. You feel like you're a liability to your team, and the fear of fumbling infects every move you make on the field because you're filled with dread that the other shoe is gonna drop. Before our Week 4 game against the Jets, I was quoted in the *New York Times* as saying I was "depressed" about my fumbling and that I was having bad dreams about it.

The mental intensity of the pro game was another thing to adjust to. Every game, there's so much pressure because so much is on the line. Every time guys go out there, they can suffer a permanent injury.

Every time, they can lose their livelihood and get thrown back to the situations they came from—and many of those situations are bad.

Nobody wants the dream to die, and guys did what they had to do to keep it alive, week by week. I remember being shocked early in my rookie year to see guys in the locker room taking shots of whiskey, drinking beers, and smoking down a few cigarettes at halftime. Guys did coke in the bathroom. Guys took uppers, guys took pain pills. Almost every guy did *something*. Soon enough I'd understand: playing in an NFL game is an unnatural thing to ask a human being to do, and we were all trying to get our minds to a place where it's possible to perform the way we need to. Starting in my second year, after an injury to my toe, I took a Darvocet, a painkiller. It helped my toe but the benefit was also mental: it calmed my nerves and allowed me to get through the violence of the next three hours.

Steroids were prevalent—you'd see syringes in guys' lockers—and they worked. You could identify the guys juicing—in the locker room, you could tell by their physiques; on the field, you could tell because running into them was like hitting a stone wall. I was big and fast and strong enough with the ability God gave me, but a lot of guys weren't, and steroids gave them the ability to stay in the league and have success. Like I said, on a week-to-week basis, guys did what they had to do to survive.

So those first three games I scuttled along. I wasn't discouraged, but I was frustrated. If you're used to a certain level of success, it feels *unnatural* to struggle. I needed to figure this out.

Then we got on a plane to New York again, this time to play the Jets.

LeRoy Irvin, our cornerback who became one of my close friends, told me to watch out for a corner on the Jets named Jerry Holmes. He said Holmes ran a 4.3 in the 40 and was one of the fastest guys in the league.

I shot back at LeRoy: *Shit, he ain't faster than me.*

LeRoy said he was. I said he wasn't. LeRoy said he was. I said he wasn't.

That Sunday was a perfect day at Shea Stadium, a 4 p.m. start in the late afternoon sun. We won the coin toss and took the ball. And on the second play of the game, from our 15-yard line, I took a pitch, set up a crease with a couple of hesitation stutter steps, then flew through it to daylight. My shoulders went up and back as I reached top speed, and I blew past a defensive back who took a bad angle because he'd underestimated my speed. That D-back's name was Jerry Holmes.

I was gone. Egithy-five yards for the touchdown, and right before I crossed the goal line, Holmes dove at my legs and came up empty. Out of all my highlight-reel runs, that one's probably the prettiest.

Pretty. My mom used to say that. She couldn't stand football and didn't want me to play, but when she saw me run, even she would have to give it up. *Boy, you know I hate that sport,* she'd say. *But you make it look so pretty and easy.*

Those first few weeks, nothing had been easy for me, but with that one play, football felt pretty and easy again. That one run restored my confidence. I had 192 yards in that game. I had broken out. From that point on, I knew my speed would play at the pro level, and knowing this made everything click into place.

That game turned out to be dramatic and memorable. In the third quarter, we got into a huge fight with the Jets. It actually started in a meeting that week when John Robinson told the team we weren't gonna let Mark Gastineau (talk about steroid guys) do that silly-ass sack dance he always did. Fast-forward to the third quarter, when, with the game tied at 14, Gastineau beat Jackie Slater for a sack and broke into the dance. Jackie chased him down and shoved him from behind, mid-dance, and all hell broke loose after that. It took the refs several minutes to get everything under control, and the fact that so many of our guys jumped in showed how close we were as a team. I squared off against a D-back and was pounding on him. It was the first fight of my career and was another instance in that game where I felt I was finally getting into the swing of things.

Later on in the game was what I call my "a-ha moment." This was the one play where I really felt like I belonged, that I was doing what I was put on Earth to do. Everything about that play is as vivid in my mind now as it was decades ago.

It was the fourth quarter, and we were behind by a touchdown. It was dusk outside, the stadium lights were on, and I remember looking into the distance and seeing the fog at the bottom of the lights. Vince Ferragamo called a pass play in the huddle where I was supposed to run a swing route. As we broke the huddle, Vince caught my eye. Vince was always cool but serious, the type of quarterback for whom no moment is ever too big. He told me: *If I don't see anything downfield, I'm coming to you.*

I ran the pattern I was supposed to, a slow developing route. When I looked back I saw the Jets rushers pushing back our offensive linemen, forming a green circle around Vince. I could only see the Rams horns on his helmet going from side to side as he scanned the field. Then I saw his arm come forward and over the top. It was a tight spiral, to me.

I swear, when that ball was in the air, everything I'd been through and worked for came flashing across my mind all at once. I was so grateful. I was in awe. I thought: *Damn! I'm in the NFL!*

I caught the ball for a 20-something-yard gain. It kept a key drive alive. We'd score a touchdown a few plays later to tie the game, though we'd lose the game in overtime.

But that play: I still can't get over how that felt. In that one play, football became fun again. After that play, I had the feeling I was about to accomplish some great things.

◆

Seven days later, back in Anaheim to play the Lions, I rushed for 199 yards on 30 carries. That made it 192 yards against the Jets and 199 against the Lions, and a few days later, the Rams PR guy called me in and said I was gonna be on the cover of *Sports Illustrated.*

At first, I assumed I'd share the cover with a bunch of other guys. But no, it was just me: I was running with high knees, busting through an arm tackle, with the California sun making my goggles, mouthpiece, and the yellow horn on my helmet pop. The text on the cover said "Running Wild!" For any athlete, especially back then, being on the cover of *SI* was a dream come true. All those people back in Sealy that said I wouldn't amount to anything; all those writers that called me a bust my freshman year: What did they think of me when they went to the newsstand that week?

I'd heard about the *SI* cover jinx, but I didn't believe in any of that. The next week I went for 142, then dropped down to 64, then went back up to 144, and by that point I was the favorite for Rookie of the Year. After that 85-yarder against the Jets, I was "running wild" for sure. Having confidence in my speed was a huge reason why. Once I knew that the game wasn't too fast for me, my timing slid into place.

Stardom came quick. That's the way it is in L.A. Suddenly, there I was at the Forum at Inglewood, getting a standing ovation at a Lakers game. Magic, Kareem, and their teammate Michael Cooper all came over at different points in the game and said what's up. There I was, going to parties at Magic's house. There I was, getting VIP treatment at Carlos'n Charlie's, the hot club in L.A. back then for Black celebrities. There were beautiful women there, of all races. In Texas, you had to watch yourself if you talked to a white girl. In L.A., you could talk to anybody. When I started getting out and around in L.A., I felt free in a way I never had before.

I talked about my a-ha moment *on* the field against the Jets, when it snapped into clarity that—*damn!*—I was in the NFL. Off the field, I had a bunch of those too. One time, this drop-dead gorgeous girl came up to me at Carlos'n Charlie's.

She goes: *When are me and you gonna get together?*

Without missing a beat, I go: *How 'bout right now?*

Next thing I know, we're walking out of the club together into an alley. We fucked right there by a tree, with people walking by and everything. Then we went back into the club like it was no big thing. That was L.A. Sex was just in the air.

In college, in Texas, the girls made you work for it. They wanted to date you, they wanted a commitment. L.A. was completely different, especially when you had some celebrity. I remember after a game once, walking out of the stadium with a bunch of teammates I was gonna go to the club with, and this gorgeous girl comes up to me and goes, *Hold up, sweetheart. I will suck your dick like you've never had it sucked.* The guys were like, *Go with her! Go with her!* But I didn't. The sex was that easy—it truly was the land of milk and honey. Everything was free.

That went for drugs, too: in the early '80s, in L.A., drugs were as out in the open as sex was. You'd walk into the bathroom and see people doing coke like it was no big thing. I'd never seen drugs before coming to L.A. and, frankly, I was scared of them. I didn't touch drugs for the same reason I wasn't a big drinker: I never liked the feeling of not being in control, and my mom would've whooped my ass if she ever heard about me and drugs. And with the amount of women available, I was covered in terms of vices.

Case in point: the first time I ever saw cocaine was at a bachelor party in Laguna Beach. There were women everywhere, and then the coke came out and they were passing it around on a glass plate. When it came to me, Gary Jeter, a veteran defensive end who had a good, long career as a pass rusher, said, *Naw, Rookie, don't do that.*

Instead, I got a blow job. That was good enough for me.

I had a sense that guys didn't peer pressure me because they knew what kind of talent I had and they'd seen how drugs could derail a career. That had happened to my backfield mate, Robert Alexander, a talented player whose drug use was running him out of the league. Another teammate of mine years later, Charles White, had a decent career but fell way short of his potential because of drugs.

So I stayed away. And as my rookie season went on, after I'd gotten a taste of L.A., I really just wanted to get through the season without making any big mistakes. I wanted to enjoy being young, sure, but not at the expense of doing what I loved to do, which was playing football.

And there was a lot more football to play.

◆

The week after the Detroit game that landed me on the cover of *SI*, we went to San Francisco. It was my initiation into our rivalry with the 49ers.

Guys were *up* for that game. The intensity at the facility that week was different from anything I'd seen. In the NFL, players are professionals, and unlike with the fans, you don't usually see personal bad feelings toward opposing teams outside of the competition of the game. That wasn't the case with us and San Fran: our guys *hated* them, in a way you don't see nowadays in the free-agency era. That 49ers team was smart and great, but they were dirty: late hits from their defensive guys and chop blocks from their offensive guys weren't just one-offs that occasionally happened. They were part of their system.

Us versus the Niners was a contrast in styles: they were finesse, we were power. They were pretty, we were tough. They got all the national pub, we felt overlooked. They had won a Super Bowl and would win a few more, and we hadn't, and wouldn't.

Guys told me that when we came out onto the field at Candlestick Park, I should keep my helmet on and my head down. True enough, when we came out of the tunnel, the fans started throwing bottles and other shit at us. They'd thrown stuff at our bus when we pulled in. During warmups, they were screaming and cursing at us. If I didn't get it before then, I got it now: L.A. and San Francisco don't like each other. That whole laid-back West Coast reputation? It didn't apply to our rivalry.

That first game in San Fran was a Rams-style game. Our running game pushed around their defense, which was fast and good but small. We ran for nearly 200 yards, and I had 142. With our offense playing ball control, our defense shut down Joe Montana in a 10–7 win.

Two weeks later we met again back in Anaheim, with both teams 5–2. Through three quarters, we outplayed them, and early in the fourth, we went up 35–24 after tight end Mike Barber caught a touchdown pass. I was feeling good, and on the sideline after that play, I told Mike, *I think we got this.*

Mike shook his head sternly: *As long as they got number 16 over there, it ain't over.*

He was right. Montana was unconscious the rest of the way. The 49ers won 45–35, and I couldn't believe what had hit us.

That was my first brush with Joe Montana and Bill Walsh's West Coast offense, which was years ahead of what other teams were doing at the time. I had never even heard of a timing route before, and seeing Montana throw the ball before guys were even out of their breaks blew my mind. At that time, everyone—including our defense—had no answer for stuff like that.

Something else that amazed me: in a team meeting, one of our defensive coaches said the 49ers' receivers would run routes in the first half specifically to set up routes later in the game. That's how choreographed everything was: guys who weren't the primary receivers would give the D-backs a look on a play just so they could do something different later where they *were* the primary receiver.

Bill Walsh really was a cut above everyone else. I gained an appreciation for that when he coached me in the Pro Bowl. The complexity of the system, including the choice routes running backs ran in the passing game, made it obvious that he was playing chess while the rest of the league was playing checkers.

Of course, that perception pissed off other coaches—including John Robinson, who had a huge chip on his shoulder about Walsh: *He's not that fucking smart*, was what he'd always say. I get where John was coming from: First, John was the head coach at USC when Walsh was the head coach at Stanford, and John got the best of him in those years. Second, John's knowledge of the running game—the intricacies, the angles—was on par with Bill's knowledge of the passing game, and nobody wrote a biography about John called *The Genius*.

But Walsh *was* that smart. I loved John as a coach, and it's no knock on him to say this, but he wasn't quite on Walsh's level. The 49ers moved the ball with such ease. With us everything was methodical. I've always thought I could've accomplished a lot more as a receiver in Walsh's offense, where the running backs were used as pass-catchers. My rookie year, I had 51 catches for 404 yards, but I never had more than 26 catches and 205 yards in any year after that.

The frustrating thing about our rivalry with the Niners was that if you take away Walsh and Montana, we had more talent on our roster than they did. In the eight games I played against them as a Ram, we went 3–5, with many of those losses coming down to a play here or there. To watch them pile up those Super Bowls while we couldn't even get to one haunts me to this day.

I would've loved the chance to play them in the playoffs, and one of the things that pisses me off most about getting traded by the Rams in my prime is that I didn't get that opportunity. The Rams finally had the chance in 1989, in the NFC Championship game, but the Niners won that game 30–3.

I talked to Jackie Slater about that game and he told me a story: On the flight home from San Francisco, John called him over when Jackie was walking down the aisle. Jackie had been with the Rams since 1976—and would stay with them through 1995—so he was basically an honorary coach. John was down in the dumps. He prided himself on running the football, but the Rams only had 26 rushing yards that day. Jackie told me the O-line was opening up big holes but running back Greg Bell just wasn't hitting them. The final score was lopsided, but if the Rams could have had a guy to maximize those holes, that game's a different story. So John was depressed, and wistful. He told Jackie: *If we would've had one guy, we would've won that game. If we would've had number 29 . . .*

I think about that a lot. My whole career with the Rams, our roster was championship-caliber except we didn't have a quarterback. Then, by the time Jim Everett developed—he led the league in touchdown passes in '88 and '89—what the Rams needed was a great running back.

◆

Before all those disappointments, though? Before things went south with the Rams? I was just happy to be there. I loved football. I loved my teammates. I loved playing for John Robinson. I loved being in the NFL—and my first year was an around-the-league tour of all the great players.

After our loss at home against San Francisco, we played the Dolphins in Miami, where Dan Marino had started to light it up. I'd met and liked Dan when I played against him in the Cotton Bowl in my last college game, and we have a good relationship to this day. I got drafted at the top of the first round, he got drafted at the bottom, but by the time we played each other, we were the frontrunners for Rookie of the Year award and a lot of teams were kicking themselves for not drafting Dan.

He sliced us up in that game and it was something to watch: his release was incredibly quick and fluid. He was as natural at throwing the ball as I was running with it. He was one of those athletes who, even when he's on the other side, is a joy to watch because, like me, he makes it look pretty and easy.

Our next game was against the Chicago Bears, in Anaheim. That week in practice, John Robinson told the guys on defense that if anyone took a cheap shot or had a late hit against Walter Payton, they'd get fined. That made an impression on me: Walter had earned that much respect. I wanted to be respected like that too.

During the game, LeRoy Irvin had Walter pinned in along the sideline, and he pulled up because he didn't want to risk getting a personal foul. But if you know Walter's running style, you know that wasn't wise: Walter was famous for never giving up on a play and for dishing out punishment along the sideline. When LeRoy pulled up, Walter stiff-armed him and knocked him on his ass. LeRoy staggered back to the sideline all pissed off, muttering to himself, *Man, fuck this shit!*

I went for 127 yards in that game. With the exception of our loss in the '85 NFC Championship game, I always played well against the Bears. That was a tough defense but we were a tough offense, and it pisses me off that even though we beat them three of the four times we played them when I was there, the only game most people remember is the playoff game. After our game my rookie year, I went up to Walter and said, *I'm Eric Dickerson.*

—*I know who you are*, he said, just like Magic had said to me a couple months earlier.

Walter was cool and down-to-earth, and over the years, mostly from being in Hawaii for Pro Bowls together, we became good friends. He was a fun guy and a great practical joker.

When he decided to retire years later, I asked him why, because he still had a lot left in the tank. He told me that he couldn't stand Mike Ditka and just couldn't play another season for him. Ditka said all the right things in public about Walter, but Walter told me Ditka was full of shit and was trying to push him out. I think Walter never got over the way Ditka did him in Super Bowl XX, when he denied him the chance to score a touchdown even when the Bears were blowing out the Patriots and piling on touchdowns. Ditka claimed he just forgot about Walter, but Walter never believed that, and I don't either.

When Walter got sick, I talked to him three weeks before he passed away. I feel fortunate for that. We had a funny conversation:

—*How you doing, Walter?*

—*Just trying to live.*

—*I saw you on TV. Do reporters still ask you stupid-ass questions?*

—*Yeah. The other day, one asked me if I was afraid to die. I said, "Hell yeah. I've never died before."*

The week after the Bears game, we played Atlanta on Monday Night Football. I was taking the elevator from the stadium to the locker room area, and when the door opened, I saw Howard Cosell standing right there. That's the way my rookie year was: all these guys I knew from TV, all of a sudden I was seeing them in the flesh.

Cosell didn't disappoint.

—*Ehhh-ric Dick-uh-son. Running back. South-uhn Methodist University. How's it going, Eric?*

—*How's it going Howard?*

—*Now, lemme ask you a question: How in the hell did you and Craig James split time there at SMU? What the hell were they thinking down there? What the hell was going on?*

I told him it was just how they did things down there.

—*Lemme tell you something: he should thank his lucky stars that he got to play with a guy like you. He had no business being on the field with you.*

I changed the subject, telling him that I was a big fan of his and I was excited he was doing one of my games.

◆

Splitting carries with Craig was ultimately a good thing for me because it saved my body. But during my rookie year, the fact that I'd never been asked to carry the load for an offense meant that in the last five games or so, I was getting tired and hitting that "rookie wall."

The college season was twelve games, while the NFL's was sixteen, plus four preseason games, plus the grueling training camp that began two weeks early for rookies. It was all taking its toll on me: my weight dropped from 225 at the beginning of the season to 212 by the end.

Going into camp, I had no idea that John Robinson would build the offense around me, but that year, I gained 40 percent of the Rams' total yards while leading the league in touches with 441. That workload is unheard of in today's game: the last five league leaders in touches have had 397, 403, 381, 406, and 373.

The whole team began to sputter a bit the last few weeks of the season. We were 8–5, needing just one more win to make the playoffs and with the chance to win the division if we won out, but we pissed away the next two games. First, we lost in Philly, where the fans were as nasty and disgusting as their reputation—I got pelted with a battery during a postgame interview—then we lost at home against New England, a team that for some reason always gave us trouble.

The two losses took us out of the running for the division and set up a win-or-go-home game in New Orleans against the Saints, who had the same record as us and were in the exact same position.

That might have been the most intense game I ever played in. The Saints had never made the postseason before and their fans were *starving* for the playoffs. The Superdome atmosphere was delirious, with all the voodoo and the Mardi Gras beads and the *Who dat?* chants. In other words, it was the opposite of the sparse, passive crowds we usually had in Anaheim, where the noise would just drift out of the stadium into the mild air. The Superdome was insanely loud—we had to use a silent count—and the roof just bottled in all the noise and tension.

The game came down to our final drive. We got the ball trailing

24–23 and needed to move into field goal range. It was loud as hell and everything was on the line, but Vince Ferragamo was calm and cool in the huddle. That was what was great about Vinny, who I consider the best quarterback I ever played with. He'd been battered all day by a tough Saints defense, but on the last drive he was at his best, completing six of seven passes to take us down the Saints' 25-yard line.

On came Mike Lansford, our barefooted kicker—remember those guys?—who knocked in a 42-yarder as time expired. It was one of the sweetest moments in my career. The crowd that had been so loud all game went dead silent, and all you could hear were our guys yelling and screaming on the sideline. We were headed to Dallas to play the Cowboys in the Wild Card game.

I had struggled the previous few games and didn't play great against the Saints, but I didn't care. The only thing that mattered was that we were going to the playoffs. That's the thing about that Rams locker room in those years: nobody gave a shit about their stats. It was all about team and all about winning.

What a year it had been. I was going to the playoffs to play the Dallas Cowboys back in Texas Stadium, the stadium where I'd been a star just the year before.

◆

It was a cold day in Dallas. After being exhausted the past several weeks, I found a second wind.

I wanted this game badly. I'd always hated the Cowboys.

Recall the scrimmage against the Cowboys before the season, when I forgot all my plays and had to be pulled from the action. Before the scrimmage, Tom Landry had told John Robinson that he didn't think I'd make a good pro because I ran too upright, a familiar and tired knock on me. To his credit, Landry changed his tune after the scrimmage and told John that I'd be just fine. But John told me what he'd said and I never forgot it.

My disdain for the Cowboys stretched back all the way to my

childhood. The arrogance of calling themselves "America's Team." The whole way they were into their *system* and their computers, as if the players were just widgets. I remembered from my childhood when the organization went to war with running back Duane Thomas, and how they did him dirty and dragged his name through the mud. (Long before my own contract disputes, I'd known I'm someone who instinctively sides with labor in conflicts with management.)

I also never cared for the arrogance of the city of Dallas. As a guy from Sealy, I knew that Dallas people looked down on us, just like they look down on the whole rest of the state. Sealy's located in the Houston area, and Houston and Dallas don't mix, just like the friction between L.A. and San Francisco or New York and Boston. Dallas is white-collar and Houston is its blue-collar cousin. They see us as a bunch of roughnecks and hicks. We see them as a bunch of arrogant assholes.

That's basically how we thought of those Cowboys teams. They went 12–4 that year and the mystique of their '70s dominance was still there, and we had been 9–7. But we thought they were fading, and soft, and that we could establish the run against them. Their flex defense was easy for me to run against because their interior linemen played a yard off the line of scrimmage and engaged our guards so they could read the direction of the play. Against me, that didn't work because of my acceleration. By the time their linemen read the play, I had blown past them.

That playoff game wasn't my best game—I had 23 carries for 99 yards—but it was better than previous weeks and it was good enough, and we beat the Cowboys in their own place, 24–17. I'm telling you, it felt good. I remember the sight of those pissed-off Cowboys fans leaving that stadium, shocked their elite Cowboys had lost to a 9–7 team.

I had my first playoff win under my belt—but what happened after the game reminded me that I was still a young kid with a lot to learn about life in the NFL. I was doing an interview in the locker room when David Hill came up to me and told me that two women were having a fistfight outside the door. I knew exactly what was going on: I'd dated a girl in college, Christine, a white girl from Plano, Texas, and she'd asked me to get her tickets for the game. Trouble was, I flew in my girlfriend, Monique, who was Black, and I got her tickets too. (I'd dated Monique in college as well.) After the game, both had somehow gotten down to the locker room area.

When I came out, I saw Christine in a rage. Her makeup and mink coat were all messed up and she kept screaming at Monique, *I'm gonna sue you! I'm gonna sue you!*

Nowadays, somebody would take a video of that and it would go viral, and they'd write about a thousand articles about "Karens" and white privilege. Back in '83, it was just a wake-up call that I had to be more careful with women. Welcome to the NFL, Rook.

◆

Our season ended in Washington the next week. There's not too much to say: that '83 Washington team was a juggernaut even though they wound up losing the Super Bowl to the Raiders. We ran into a buzzsaw and got demolished, 51–7.

It was cold as hell and we fell behind 24–0 by the second quarter. RFK Stadium was packed and *loud*. The place had a raw, crazy energy. The stands were so close to the field I thought they were gonna cave in and fall on us.

Washington had a huge advantage over us because the field was frozen, and we had only brought our long cleats that normally dug into the grass but provided no traction on the frozen field. Meanwhile, Washington was wearing turf shoes, which were flat, so their guys had much better footing.

Another advantage they had was that the heat was cut off in our locker room, which I have no doubt was intentional. Guys had their jackets on during our pregame meeting and nobody wanted to take them off to get dressed. The showers were all cold water, too. It was just a miserable day, and when we were getting blown out and it became clear we weren't coming back, all I could think of was that I couldn't wait for it to end. All of the mental and physical exhaustion set in when

I was freezing my ass off on the bench.

When it was over, I thought about everything I'd accomplished that season. We'd gone from a record of 2–7 in the previous strike-shortened season to the divisional round of the playoffs. I'd set a rookie record with 1,808 rushing yards, which I don't think will ever be broken. Because I set the all-time rushing record the following year, that '83 season gets overlooked, but it was almost as productive. I had 404 receiving yards, so I led the league with 2,212 yards from scrimmage compared to 2,244 in '84. I made All-Pro, won Rookie of the Year, and finished second in the MVP voting to Joe Theismann.

This surprises a lot of people, but I consider the rookie record the one that's harder to break than the single-season mark of 2,105. It wouldn't shock me if someone broke 2,105, but no one's breaking the 1,808. Rookies are simply not prepared to handle that kind of workload. I would know, because I really wasn't either.

It wasn't just the physical exhaustion, it was everything else: I'd never lived on my own and paid bills and taxes before. I'd never been a *celebrity* before. By the end of the year, when I'd go out, I'd get mobbed. I'd get stared at, which made me uncomfortable. At first the attention was cool, but it became too much. It was a great season but I learned I didn't want to be a mega-celebrity. I needed a break.

Afterward, I resolved to myself that next season I'd be prepared for it all. I resolved that I wouldn't wear down.

I went back to Sealy to catch my breath. I mostly spent the off-season laying low and hanging with the guys I grew up with. I went to Houston to see relatives and chase girls. Life's weird: everything had changed, but nothing had.

That offseason, I was talking to my friend Gary Hill's brother, Henry, and the topic of Magic Johnson came up. I told him I knew him, that we were friendly, and that I'd actually been to his house.

—*What? Come on, Eric! You lying. You don't know Magic Johnson!*

—*Henry, I'm telling you. You gotta think: I was All-Pro…*

—*Nah, you lying. You ain't even on that level!*

I don't blame him for not believing it. I hardly could either.

CHAPTER 8

2,105

Here are a couple of surprising things about my stellar sophomore year, when my 2,105 rushing yards broke the record for most ever in a single season.

First: the offseason before, I got fat. I was so wiped out from my rookie year that I sat on my ass and ate. I ballooned to 250 pounds.

But it didn't matter. I was such a freak of nature in those days that I went to the track at Sealy High, hit the weight room, and was back down to 222 in two weeks. My body was cut and I was ready to go.

Second: that season—and in fact my career—almost ended in Week 8 against the Falcons. The first part of the year had been good: 780 yards through seven games, on pace for 1,783. But late in the game against the Falcons, a guy tackling me landed on the back of my foot, which was perpendicular to the ground. That placed all of our combined weight on my right big toe, and I heard a cracking sound. I played through it but minutes later my toe had swelled up so much it was putting pressure on my shoe. I was sure it was broken, but the X-ray the next day showed it was turf toe.

Big deal, I thought. *Big deal*, a lot of people think when they think of turf toe. It's just a toe, one of the smallest body parts it's possible to injure.

I was wrong.

People laugh when I tell them this, but it was the most painful, debilitating injury I've ever had. Picture someone cutting your toe open, putting glass in it, and saying, *Okay, now walk*. It hurts to this day. Not long ago, I was playing golf and I dropped a ball on it and it felt like a fucking anvil. I was howling in agony and had to sit down for a few minutes.

Before our next game against San Francisco, I got it drained and I got injections, and the trainers taped it, but it didn't matter. I was in severe pain and I couldn't push off that toe. I was making my cuts off the side of my foot, thinking about every step. I was hobbling while defenders were flying. It was dangerous for me to be out there. I had 38 yards that game.

A couple days later, Gary Tuthill, our trainer, saved my career. That's no exaggeration. To rush for 2,105 yards and to have the career I had, you have to have a lot of people helping you along the way. Without Gary Tuthill, you probably would have forgotten about Eric Dickerson.

He passed away a long time ago, but it's time he gets his due. He was a short, squat guy who was funny and gruff. The players respected and trusted him. Some trainers just want to get you back on the field, but Tuthill wanted to get you *healthy*.

Tuthill had an idea for my toe: he sent me to a lab to take a wax molding of my foot. Using that, he designed a toe piece for me. Made of hard plastic with a cushion inside, it went around my whole toe and somehow took all that pressure off it.

After I started wearing it, I still felt some pain but I could cut normally again. That week, playing against the St. Louis Cardinals, I busted out, rushing for 208 yards. The next several weeks I had 149, 132, 191, 149, and 215. With Tuthill's toe piece, I was off and running into the record books.

◆

It's hard for me to put into words how much I loved football my first couple years in the league. Early in my career, in practice, I had one of those moments where you step outside yourself. We had just broken the huddle and I was walking to the line of scrimmage. The weather was perfect, 70 and sunny. And it hit me: *Man, I'm in the NFL . . .*

It hit me how much I loved it. It hit me that it wouldn't last forever, which made me love it even more.

I loved everything about being a pro football player. I loved the women and the money. I loved the smell of the grass and the camaraderie of the locker room.

But mostly I loved the feeling of running. I loved the feeling of the breeze in my face. I loved hearing the roar of the crowd as background noise, but mostly hearing the sound of my breathing through my mouthpiece. I loved seeing the goalposts get closer and closer. It felt like I wasn't even running my hardest, and that there was no top speed I could reach. Everything was so smooth and natural, as if I were put on Earth by God to run with the ball. Nothing in my life before or since has ever given me as much joy as I felt running with the ball.

My talent was in my genes. Before that Cardinals game, my first with the toe piece, Emmitt Thomas, an assistant coach with the Cardinals, came up to me. He'd gone to Bishop College, a historically Black school in Texas.

—*Is your father Richard Seals?*

I was floored. I said yeah, he was my biological dad. Thomas said that he'd played college ball against him when Richard played at Prairie View A&M. He said he remembered his running style—upright, smooth, gliding—and that when he saw highlights of me, he had déjà vu.

A lot has been made about my upright running style. It was always held against me, like when Landry questioned why the Rams had drafted me. Recently, I came across an old scouting report that said, *Negatives: Runs too upright.*

Here's the thing people don't understand: yes, I ran upright, but I only did that once I broke into the open field. When I came through the line of scrimmage, or if I was in traffic, I wasn't running with my chest exposed. I came out low and fast. That's something that made me special. A lot of big guys can't accelerate and it's not natural for them to run low. They'll bend themselves into an unathletic position where they lose their burst. Not me.

It worked for me because I have really good feet. People ask me what my best attribute as a runner was, and that's what I tell them. When you have good feet, you're balanced when the defenders aren't, and your body is always in a good position to do the next thing. When you have good feet, you can change directions smoothly, without slowing down as much: it's subtle and hard to capture on TV, but you can tell the difference when you're in the middle of the action.

I was a *smooth* athlete. My feet were smooth, my gait was smooth. Everything was efficient, relaxed. And when you're smooth, you have the element of deception, because you're not telegraphing your next move like the choppy guys do. When you're smooth, you can accelerate past guys without them knowing until it's too late. Again, it's a subtle thing: Tom Landry, or whoever wrote that scouting report, wouldn't have been able to see it.

Neither would a lot of coaches. Ever since I started playing, I had coaches who tried to change my running style. I'd always give them a short nod—*Uh huh, okay*—but I wouldn't pay it any mind. I knew myself better as an athlete than they knew me.

Because I was so fluid, people always underestimated how fast I was. During one of my first practices in training camp in '83, I was carrying the ball and John Robinson blew the whistle.

—*Stop, stop, stop. Eric, on this play, you can't be jogging.*

—*Coach, I'm not jogging.*

I told him I was going faster than he thought: *Get out here and try to catch me*, I said.

Fast-forward a few weeks to that Jets game, when I broke that 85-yard touchdown run. On the sideline, John came up to me and said, *I guess you* weren't *jogging.*

People's eyes told them I wasn't that fast: that happened all the time. My rookie year, LeRoy Irvin challenged me to a race. We raced after practice and I beat him easily.

At a club, a random guy challenged me: *Man, I see you on TV, you ain't that fast. I bet I can outrun you.* I gave him a five-yard head start and beat him easily. I told him what I always used to say to people: *Don't let that TV fool you.*

I was one of those athletes that made it look easy. I have no doubt this played into the public perception of me. To a lot of people, I was a Black guy making lots of money while going three-quarter speed who had the audacity to complain he was underpaid.

But who gives a shit what they thought? I was fast and explosive, and that set up my whole game. Defenders were afraid of my speed, which meant they were always overrunning plays. My whole thing was feeling out the hips of the defenders: If they turned their hips to chase me to the outside, it gave me a lane to cut back through. If they didn't, I could feel they were a beat behind, and I'd accelerate past them.

I had a *feel* for running. People often use the term *vision*, but what they really mean is *feel*. Feel is vision combined with anticipation. It's knowing how the play will unfold before it unfolds. In '84, I had developed a feel for NFL defenses and also for my offensive line.

Just as in my last year at SMU, I felt like a man playing against boys. And I loved it. I don't mean to brag, but it's an amazing feeling knowing your athletic ability—your size, your speed, your cutting—is superior. My mom had always said I made the sport look *pretty and easy*. I have to say, some of those games, it *was* easy.

My mom never bothered to learn anything about the sport, but she gave me a piece of advice about running the football that I took to heart. In high school, whenever we'd get near the goal line, my coach would always call a QB sneak so that our white quarterback would score a touchdown and not me. Even though I'd pile up rushing yards, sometimes I wouldn't score touchdowns, so my name wouldn't get in the paper and I'd be disappointed.

—*What's that called when you're running away from everybody, and you score a touchdown?*

—*You mean a long run?*

—*Yeah. The "long run." Boy,* that's *what you gotta do. Always go for the "long run."*

After that, from high school through college and on up to the pros, I was always looking for the long run, on every carry. In '84, I had a lot of them.

◆

We took pride in being a running team: you played the Rams, you knew you were in for a physical game. We liked that reputation. We loved going into other teams' stadiums and coming out of the tunnel with those dark helmets and cool uniforms. We'd hear the hushed, awed voices of the fans: *There's Eric Dickerson. There's Jackie Slater.* The fans knew what the other team knew. We were gonna come into their stadium and run the ball down their throats.

The running game always carried us, but that was especially true in '84, when Vince Ferragamo broke his hand during our third game and was replaced by Jeff Kemp. Jeff was a good guy everyone liked, but he wasn't in Vince's class in terms of throwing ability. That year, I had more *rushing* yards than Jeff had *passing* yards.

Those first couple years, we'd literally pound teams into submission. You'd see it in the defenders' eyes before the play started: they wanted no part of us. There'd be a time in the game where we *knew* we had them. We came to recognize that look, and it was incredibly satisfying.

Our philosophy was simple: if you couldn't stop it, you were gonna see a heavy dose of it. Our blocking schemes were mostly go-straight-at-your-man, with some cross blocking. We didn't run many plays, but what we ran, we ran well. And we mixed things up by running them out of different sets with different motions. That was what was great about John Robinson: he didn't overcomplicate things. He knew that running the football was all about mentality and execution, and that if you made things too complicated, it would take away from your players' aggressiveness.

Our signature play was 47 Gap (46 Gap if we ran it to the right side). Without getting into the details of the blocking scheme, it was an attack play where our backside guard and tackle pulled so they could get a head of steam and hit someone. For me, the play gave me options: I could go inside, outside, or cut back. If teams couldn't stop 47 Gap, we'd run it until the cows came home. In 1984, that's exactly what we did.

That year, everything *worked*. The plays we ran *worked*. Every decision on every cut I made *worked*. We didn't fall behind early in games, so we stuck with the run. And unlike the year before, I was getting stronger in the second half of the season. I wasn't gonna run out of gas this time.

That offensive line was talented and cohesive, on and off the field. Those guys and I got along from the moment I showed up as a rookie. I think they knew that to get recognition as a line, they needed a great running back, just like I needed a great line to do my thing. My rookie year, I asked Jackie Slater if he'd ever been to a Pro Bowl. He told me no—and I told him that was about to change. I was right: he made seven Pro Bowls after that, made the Hall of Fame, and is on the short list of best offensive tackles of all time.

That year, I was totally in sync with them. I knew who could pull fast, who was a little slower, and who was best at holding which kind of block. Little, subtle things that can make all the difference when you're talking about fractions of a second.

They were a tremendous group of guys who I formed a lifelong bond with. White guys, Black guys, it didn't matter: we were the definition of a team. After every home game, all the linemen—except for Jackie and center Doug Smith, who were devoutly religious—would go to the Red Onion in Santa Ana. We were constantly together and we relied on each other. It was the definition of a brotherhood.

The deans, the wise vets everyone looked up to, were Jackie, our left tackle, and Dennis Harrah, our right guard. Dennis got to the Rams in '75 and Jackie got there in '76. Between them those guys would make thirteen Pro Bowls. And they couldn't have been more different from each other in terms of leadership styles.

Jackie was an extremely religious Black guy from Mississippi, a straight-arrow family man you didn't want to disappoint. He'd give us a hard time when he heard us talking about chasing women.

—*Why you talkin' about all these girls—don't you have a girlfriend?*
—*Yeah. I got a couple.*
—*That's not right—you gotta settle down!*

It got to a point where we'd stop talking about women in front of him. But in '84, before a game while he was injured, I caught him on the sideline standing perfectly still, just staring at the cheerleaders.

—*Jackie? What you looking at?*

He didn't look at me and kept staring at them.

—*Eric, those are some fine specimens of women over there.*

That was the first and last time I ever talked about women with Jackie.

Dennis was a funny old redneck from West Virginia and a six-time Pro Bowler. He had a huge head—we called him "waterhead"—and he'd always fart in the huddle. Usually, he'd time it to be as funny as possible, like when the quarterback was calling out the play, or right after we broke the huddle and were jogging to the line.

Dennis would crack off-color jokes you couldn't get away with these days, but it was cool, because he went after the white guys as well as the Black guys. I'm telling you, that group was so close. It was an example of how, in sports, when guys respect each other and enjoy each other's company, you don't *forget* color but it becomes totally irrelevant.

In '84, Jackie went down with a season-ending knee injury in Week 7. But we didn't miss a beat: Bill Bain filled in and did a great job. Billy was the classic "bad body" player, a guy with a big belly who didn't quite walk right. But he busted his ass and was tenacious with his blocks. He was a crafty vet and the type of guy you wanted in your corner.

Bill was a different kind of guy: standoffish, gruff, moody. One time earlier that year, I almost got into a fight with him in the parking lot when he almost hit me with his truck. I said, *What the fuck?* and he said, *Get the fuck outta the way!* But deep down he was a really good guy, and over the course of that year we developed the utmost respect for each other. That's the great thing about football and the type of camaraderie it can create.

The center was Doug Smith, a quiet, cerebral Christian and the best center I ever played with. He was an undrafted free agent who made six Pro Bowls and got in fourteen years in the league. He was so consistent with everything he did, and he'd always hold himself accountable: when he'd miss a block, which wasn't often, he'd say, *Eric, I'm sorry,* and I'd tell him not to worry, that it's football and these things happen. But that's why he was such a great player. Years later, in Indianapolis, our center, Ray Donaldson, had more talent than Doug but was half the player. That Rams team had lots of guys like Doug, and I didn't realize how special that was until I'd left.

The left guard, Kent Hill, was one of my best friends on the team and a five-time Pro Bowler himself. If Bill Bain was basically a fat guy they put a football uniform on, Kent was the exact opposite: he was cut like a skilled position player, but he was six feet five and massive. Offensive linemen just don't look like that, and nobody was more impressed with Kent's physique than Kent himself. He'd parade around the locker room with his shirt off every chance he'd get, showing off his big pecs.

Kent was a ladies' man and he was always styling—or trying to. He drove a Mercedes 450SL convertible, but he was *way* too big and tall for that car. He'd sit up straight up, and when the top was down his whole head was above the level of the windshield. He looked goofy as hell.

Irv Pankey was our right tackle. We used to tease him about his body: he had this hulking upper body but these tiny, spindly legs. He was a quiet, good-natured guy who usually didn't go out with us, but we'd give him a hard time because we'd always see him out one-on-one with women.

—*Irv, why didn't you invite us?*

—*Oh man, I'm trying to do my own thing. I'm trying to keep it on the low.*

Since we were a running team, any list of our offensive linemen isn't complete without talking about our tight end, David Hill, who was one of my best friends the team, a Texas guy from San Antonio. He was a fun-loving guy who always had a smile on his face. He was married and would always make a show of pretending he had to stay home, but it took the littlest amount of arm-twisting to get him out. He was the biggest practical jokester on the team: he'd put balm in your jock and superglue in your waistband. He also had this goofy touchdown celebration where he'd stick his big ass out and shake it.

But when it came to playing, he was completely serious. He took pride in his blocking. When the play would go to his side, he'd always say to me in the huddle, *Big Daddy, stay behind me—I got you.* And sure enough, he'd always get his man.

◆

As the season went on, I was piling up huge games, one after the next. And we started winning. After the San Francisco game, where I had 38 yards playing on my bad toe, we were 5–4. Then I got my toe piece and we won five of the next six games to clinch a playoff berth.

Breaking O. J. Simpson's record of 2,003 yards was becoming a possibility, and O. J. interviewed me on TV about breaking his record. When I had met him at USC on my recruiting trip years before, I told him I wanted to break his record, and here we were.

One of those weeks, David Hill told me: *I want this 2,000 yards on my résumé.*

His résumé. That's the way all those guys saw it. That's the way *I* saw it: it was a collective accomplishment, and sharing it with those guys is what makes it so meaningful. It's not just about something I did as an individual. It's about pulling on one rope with those men. It's about how that accomplishment enriches the relationships we had with each other.

They all wanted it badly. If I only had 60, 70 yards at halftime, guys would be on each other to step it up. Jackie Slater was injured, but he was such a part of that group that *he'd* be getting in guys' faces if they missed blocks. One game, when I only had 70 or so yards at halftime, Jackie gave the guys a fiery speech: *We need more! We need to get back on pace!*

We did. And coming into our second-to-last game against Houston, with the chance to clinch a playoff spot, I needed 212 yards to break the record. Everyone thought it was gonna be the following week in San Francisco: the 49ers game would be nationally televised, and O. J. would be the analyst for NBC. But the Houston game was our last home game, and I was having my best game of the season.

We started smelling it, and so did the crowd. It became a heated game: the Oilers didn't want that record broken on them and they were doing all kinds of dirty shit. Jerry Glanville, who'd later become my head coach with the Falcons, was their defensive coordinator. He was a fake macho man, a wannabe tough guy who was actually just a little asshole, so it's no surprise they were cheap-shotting me and twisting my ankles after the whistle. There was also lingering bad blood from the '83 draft, when the Rams traded up with the Oilers to get me and I said I was grateful because I didn't see the Oilers going anywhere. That remained true.

We got into several fights with them. I got into it with their safety, Keith Bostic, and told him, *Now I gotta break this record on y'all's asses.* The intensity of the game took our adrenaline to another level. As the game went on, every play started popping: 10 yards, 15 yards, 30 yards.

With 3:22 left in the fourth quarter, we had a 27–16 lead and I needed five yards to tie it and six to break it. Jeff Kemp pointed to me in the huddle: *What play do you want?* he said.

There was no question in my mind. We were gonna break the record with the play that got us there.

—*47 Gap.*

—*47 Gap it is,* Jeff said.

I walked to the line slowly and took everything in. David Hill looked back at me, commemorating the moment.

Irv and Kent pulled and cleared out their guys. The hole was there and it was big, and I hit it. For a moment I thought I was gonna break free for a touchdown, but a guy grabbed my legs from behind. A nine-yard gain, 2,007 yards on the season, 215 for the day, and they took me out of the game after that.

It seemed like the whole team came out to the field to mob me after the play. They were as excited as I was. That, right there, is what that record means to me.

After my rookie year, I got the linemen Rolex watches. After the

'84 season, I got them rings with the number "2,105" made out of small diamonds. I wanted to show those guys that I appreciated them. I wanted to show them we were bonded for life.

•

We went 10–6 that year and made the playoffs, a one-game improvement after going 9–7 the year before. That set us up for a home playoff game against the Giants, who we'd blown out earlier in the season, 33–12. We were five-point favorites and Anaheim Stadium was packed and loud, which, frankly, wasn't the case most of the time.

The Giants were putting together the pieces on defense that would propel their championship season in 1986: L. T., Harry Carson, Leonard Marshall, Jim Burt, Carl Banks. Not surprisingly, the game was a slugfest. They held me in check in the first half, but we got things rolling in the second half, and by the fourth quarter, we'd done what we often did during that era: we'd worn them down.

We were trailing 16–10 in the fourth quarter when we marched downfield on them. I carried the ball six times for 49 yards to get us down to the 4-yard line, setting up a second-and-goal. The game had been a struggle but on that drive, I was finally feeling it. That year had been *my* year, and I wanted nothing more than to punch the ball into the end zone for my team. We had three shots at it, with the league's best running back running behind its best offensive line. I felt I'd earned the right to try to score that touchdown.

But instead of giving me the ball, John Robinson brought Dwayne Crutchfield into the game so there were two running backs, and then called a dive play—or straight-ahead run—to him. On the game's most decisive play, I was a decoy, and Leonard Marshall sniffed it out, knifed into the backfield, and dropped Dwayne for a three-yard loss. That put us in a passing situation, but we only gained a couple of yards and had to settle for a field goal. We never threatened again and lost 16–13.

It's one of the most disappointing losses of my career. In his post-game press conference, John said he was trying to *fool* the Giants. I thought: *Ain't that a bitch*. We had finally broken them doing what we'd done all year, but then we got too smart for our own good, and the only people we fooled were ourselves. I was reminded of that play years later in the Super Bowl when the Seahawks, on the Patriots' 1-yard line and needing a touchdown to win, didn't do the obvious and just give the ball to Marshawn Lynch. Instead they threw the ball for an interception.

The Giants went into San Francisco the next week. They played them tough but lost, and it gets me to this day that we didn't get that opportunity. That '84 Niners team is thought of as one of the best of all time, but we always played them tough in their place, and the way our running game was clicking that year, we definitely had a shot. Football is a game that comes down to a few plays. That's true of games, seasons, and even careers. I look back on the second-down call as one of those plays that, had it gone differently, might have changed the complexion of my career and perhaps the perception of me.

After that season, I knew our team was *this* close—but we needed a quarterback, especially after the organization traded Vince that off-season. No disrespect to Jeff, but there were things most other teams in the league could do that we just couldn't: it would be 3rd and long and we'd run the ball. The few times we'd complete a pass over 20 yards, guys would start celebrating on the sideline.

A lot of people have made the argument that our lack of a passing game was something that *helped* me get that record. In reality, that opposite is true: I was running against stacked fronts week after week. If Vince Ferragamo would've stayed healthy and given us the ability to keep defenses honest, I firmly believe I'd have had 2,500 or 2,600 yards.

It had been a great first two seasons, but making the playoffs wasn't gonna be good enough going forward. Individual accomplishments weren't gonna be good enough going forward. I needed the Rams to get a quarterback and make a commitment to winning. And because my contract paid me like an unproven rookie rather than a guy who'd just had the two best running back seasons of all time, I needed them to make a commitment to me.

They might not have been my biological mom and dad, but nobody had better, more loving parents than I did. My mom, Viola Dickerson, and my dad, Kary Dickerson, had completely opposite temperaments, but they balanced each other out perfectly.

My biological mom, Helen Johnson, pictured with my stepdad, Robert "Bobcat" Johnson. I grew up thinking Helen was my older sister, but finding out the complicated truth didn't change how much we cared about each other.

Growing up in Sealy, Texas, there wasn't much for kids to do. My mom knew how dangerous the world could be, so she sheltered me, forbidding me to go past the streetlight on our dirt road.

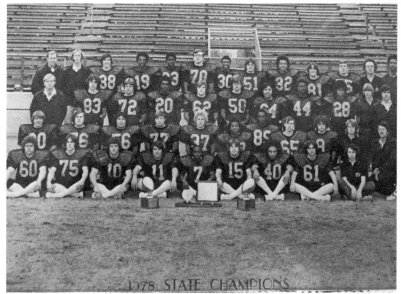

The 1978 Texas 2A State Champion Sealy Tigers. In all my years in football, this was the most close-knit team I ever played on. We all grew up together so we felt like a family. White, Black, it didn't matter. Everyone was tight. I'm #19 in the back row.

Craig James and I, aka The Pony Express. We split carries at SMU, which I didn't like at the time. But after I got to the pros, I was grateful for how it saved my body. Craig remains my close friend to this day.

I became famous for my rec specs, but I didn't start wearing them until my sophomore year at SMU. Before that I wore sports glasses like the ones Kurt Rambis of the Lakers wore.

Ron Meyer sold us on his SMU program, and after a rough start, we turned it around to become the best team in the country. Playing in Texas Stadium, we felt like a pro team playing against college kids.

The signature facemask I wore — with the two bars coming down outside the eyes — was a prototype they developed just for me, but now it's widely used. Here I am with the facemask, the neck roll, the mouth guard, the tape, the towel. Look good, feel good, play good.

Here I am with a friendly fan outside of Colts practice — I was nursing an injury at the time and they made me ride a bicycle around. This fan was cool, but my relationship with the Indianapolis fans was tumultuous.

Charles Drayton became my best friend after I met him during my freshman year at SMU. Our relationship is based on honesty — we hold nothing back from each other. He's the godfather of my children, just like I am to his.

I owe my dear friend Hollie Frey many things — possibly even my life. Hollie convinced me the neck injury I suffered in 1992, which ultimately ended my career, was serious. If not for her, I would've pushed through it. God knows what would have happened.

L.A. royalty right here. Tommy Lasorda was a friend of mine and a great
ambassador for baseball, the Dodgers and L.A. His death in 2020 hit me hard
because he was always so full of life.

I can't begin to tell you how much respect I have for my eldest daughter, Erica. She's smart, kind, hardworking and an incredible mother to my beautiful granddaughter, Irie.

I was a proud bachelor my whole life, convinced settling down wasn't for me. And then I met Penny. Some couples just play well off each other, and that's us. She's the best partner a man could ask for and a great mother to our kids.

My kids are my life. Keri is incredibly kind-hearted. She excels in track, in volleyball, and as a visual artist. Dallis is inquisitive, hilarious and is a natural-born charmer. Oh, and he's a better natural athlete than I am.

I grew up in the segregated South, where the idea that Black people were inferior to white people was in the air we breathed. Since then, Sealy has come a long way, and so has America. But not nearly far enough.

CHAPTER 9

MY STYLE, MY GOGGLES

I don't say this to brag, but merely to state the facts: in the history of the sport, nobody has ever looked cooler on the field than me.

I'll break it down for you.

THE PADS

I wore every single pad that had been invented, for two reasons: one, I wanted to protect every area of my body; and two, I wanted to make myself look as big and imposing as possible.

Guys make a macho thing out of pretending they don't care about getting hurt. But that's for guys with something to prove, and I didn't have anything to prove. Some people would give me shit about running out of bounds rather than finishing runs with contact. *Please*. When the play's over, the play's over, and if you think squeezing out another half-yard is worth the extra hits and risk, you're not tough, you're dumb.

I wore all the pads: hip pads—which in my case were actually knee pads—with the full girdle. Knee pads. Thigh pads. Elbow pads, which you needed because of all the Astroturf fields and grass fields with dirt infields, like ours in Anaheim Stadium early in the season.

I wore a flak jacket to protect my ribs. Under my shoulder pads—the boxy, '80s ones—I wore two extra layers of padding to reinforce them and lift them up a little bit more.

I liked the feeling of looking big and I didn't feel it cost me any speed. I'm six foot three, and in my cleats and my helmet, I was about six foot five. I used to love walking out of the tunnel and hearing opposing players who'd never seen me in person say to each other in hushed tones, *Damn, that's a big running back.*

THE NECK ROLL

It had nothing to do with protection. I just liked the way it looked.

Here's proof: I customized it so that it fanned out to the middle of my shoulder pads like a *V* from behind. That was my signature touch. This gave me no protection but it looked cooler.

Fanning it out took some effort: I drilled holes in my shoulder pads and threaded a string through the plastic, and used that string to tie the neck roll in place.

I didn't wear the neck roll until my junior year of college. Craig James wore one, and he was a punishing, physical back. I liked the way it looked on him and how it seemed to add to his toughness on the field. I adopted it and put my own twist on it.

THE REC SPECS

The goggles made me look like I was from another planet, an alien come to Earth to kick ass and take names. Imposing, invincible. Some people think guys look nerdy in goggles. I looked like Darth Fucking Vader.

I have terrible vision—I've been practically blind since I was eight or nine years old—and during my first few years playing football in middle school and high school, goggles hadn't been invented yet, so I had to wear prescription glasses on the field. I'd live in fear of someone breaking my glasses and blinding me, or short of that, bending the frames so I'd have to wait four weeks for a new pair to come in the mail.

In high school, I transitioned to those thick, ugly sports goggles that Kurt Rambis and Chuck Muncie used to wear. It wasn't until college that Rec Specs came out, and they were a godsend. But they weren't perfect: they'd fog up on hot or humid days. They'd get mud and dirt on them I'd always have to wipe off. A couple times I tried contacts, but without fail, they'd pop out when I'd get hit. So Rec Specs it was.

THE FACEMASK AND MOUTH GUARD

That signature facemask, with the two bars coming down on the outside of the eyes, which became the most popular in the NFL, was a prototype made specially for me. Before that, I wore the facemask with one bar coming down the middle, but I always found that distracting and it gave me a headache.

My new facemask felt freeing. I've heard that a lot of contemporary players call it "The Deion," believing that Deion Sanders wore it first. But no—Deion got it from me. As a matter of fact, toward the end of my career, when he was a rookie, Deion introduced himself to me before a game. He came running over to me and said, *Big fan! Big fan! I love the way you wear your gear, man.*

The mouth guard was the big one, which covered my entire mouth. I looked *bad*. Everything about the way I looked said, *Don't fuck with me.*

THE HELMET

A word about that old Rams helmet: it was the coolest helmet ever created. The shape of the ram horn, the way the yellow popped . . . (Don't even get me started on the weak-ass new helmet—I've made it clear I'm not a fan.)

I wore a reinforced helmet made by BIKE, which gave me extra protection. I could also tighten it by blowing up the air inside of it, which helped keep my goggles from sliding around.

THE TOWEL AND TAPE

I wrote earlier that I admired Billy Sims and the way his towel hung down from his pants, and that seeing how cool Billy looked made me want to play for Oklahoma. I didn't wind up going to OU but I adopted the towel, which I wore on my right side. Mostly, it was for style purposes, but I'd occasionally wipe off my goggles with it.

I also wore lots of tape: I had the trainers "spat" my ankle to prevent it from rolling over. Then I had them tape my wrists because it looked cool.

THE JHERI CURL

Curls for the girls, we'd say, because it was the '80s, and, I'm telling you, the women were into the Jheri curl.

People joke about how much they were supposedly paying me at SMU, but I'll give you proof of how *little* they were paying me: When I was in college, I used the S-Curl, which ran you about $20 a bottle. It wasn't until I turned pro that I could afford the $80 Jheri curl, the top-shelf product.

I got it done from a guy named Gene, in Costa Mesa. The treatment took about an hour and a half and it lasted for about four to six weeks. The best part was you could wash your hair after the game and just touch it up afterward with the activator, which is not possible for all those guys today with the long-ass dreadlocks, trying to look like the Predator.

NUMBER 29

When I was in high school, there were two obvious choices for my number: 32, because my favorite player was O. J. Simpson, and 34, the number worn by Earl Campbell, the king of Texas running backs.

But I wanted to be my own man and to wear a number nobody had seen on a running back before. I was a unique back, I wanted a unique number. My sophomore year of high school, I chose 19 and wore that throughout high school and at SMU.

In the pros, after I got drafted, I asked for 19, but the equipment guys told me I couldn't wear that. They gave me the options of 29, 25, and 32, and I chose 25. There's a photo of me in the *L.A. Times* at my introductory press conference holding up a number 25 jersey.

But it didn't sit right. Twenty-nine felt more like 19, so I told the equipment guys I'd changed my mind, and I never looked back.

CHAPTER 10

LIVING IT UP IN L.A.—FROM BEHIND THE ORANGE CURTAIN

The Rams played in the L.A. Coliseum for more than thirty years, but in 1980, they left for Anaheim Stadium, thirty miles but a world away. It was the worst decision the franchise ever made.

The Rams had been L.A.'s team for decades, going back to the days of "Night Train" Lane and "Crazy Legs" Hirsch. But with that single move, the franchise turned its back on the city, with all its diversity and energy. Veterans like Jack Youngblood, Jackie Slater, and Vince Ferragamo used to tell me about the rowdy crowds at the Coliseum: it was right in the hood, so there were Black people, Mexican people, blue-collar people. But at Anaheim Stadium, the crowds were white, passive, and sparse. It was suburban and too *comfortable*. Unless we were in the playoffs or playing someone like the Cowboys or 49ers, you could always see sections of empty seats. The passion was lacking.

As players, we felt walled off from everything that made L.A. great. We were stuck out in the O.C., which might as well have been middle America. We called it the "Orange Curtain." We were technically an L.A. team, but we knew we weren't on par with the Lakers or the Dodgers, two iconic franchises with worldwide followings. We were hidden behind the Orange Curtain.

And what happened a little bit after the Rams moved out of L.A.? In 1982, the Raiders moved from Oakland into the Coliseum and immediately stole our thunder. They won the Super Bowl in '83, and their star was Marcus Allen, a charismatic guy from USC. Right around that time, hip-hop culture started taking off. N.W.A and those guys embraced the Raiders' bad-boy image and made the Raiders hat famous.

Meanwhile, we became an afterthought in the city we'd once ruled. We were out there with the white people, with Disneyland and Mickey Mouse. Lemme say something about that: Disneyland is not a Black person's fantasy. It's one of many American fantasies that exclude Black people. Those old Disney movies were racist as hell.

I wasn't into rap, but I had mutual friends with a lot of guys in the rap scene and became friends with Eazy-E. This was before those guys got big; they were just young kids trying to make it. We went to dinner one night in the Valley and he was telling me about how everyone in the rap game was a Raiders fan. But he said they still all liked me: they saw me as a real brother, even though I played for the Rams. *Man, you should be a Raider,* he told me.

Moving to Anaheim was a slap in the face to the team's minority fans. It was classic white flight, because historically, the O.C. has always been the place where white people went to get away from everyone else. In the '80s, the O.C. was 80 percent white. And while it's getting more diverse now because of the Latino population, it's still a no-go zone for Black people, who are 2 percent of the population. I'll say that again because it's crazy: a huge county just outside America's second-biggest city is *2 percent Black.*

I thought a lot about all this during my holdout before the '85 season when I took a lot of racial abuse, which I'll talk about later. I thought a lot about it after I came back to Anaheim in 1989 as a member of the Colts, and the Orange County fans threw fake money at me as I was leaving the field. Ever see fans throw shit at a white player? Me neither.

So, the Rams lost a lot of fans with that move. And they lost the status as L.A.'s team. To this day, they're still trying to undo that mistake.

•

But I loved L.A.

Ever since I got here and saw mountains for the first time, and saw the mix of people and the vibrancy of the city, I was smitten. I bought my house in Calabasas in 1986 and lived here every offseason, and still live in that house. Even after I got traded to Indianapolis, I came back every chance I got. This is my city.

But the O.C. was a different story. I felt more racism in Orange County than I ever did in Texas growing up. In Texas, there was segregation, but Black and white people for the most part got along. In Orange County, there weren't any Black people for a reason, and I felt like a stranger in a strange land. I liked women of all colors, and I could *feel* people's eyes on me when I'd be with a white woman. Every Black man knows this feeling. It made me think of what my mom always said: *There are two things that don't live long in this world—dogs that chase cars and negroes that chase white girls.*

I lived in the O.C. my first few years in the league. It was a nice enough place to live, but I knew I wouldn't last. When you look around and you don't see anyone else who looks like you except your teammates, you know it's not the place for you.

My first year, I rented a place in Costa Mesa, but in my second year I bought a condo in Irvine: a three-bedroom, 2,000-square-foot split-level on a cul-de-sac in a development next to the Strawberry Farms Golf course. I was excited to own my own place for the first time, but I got into a bunch of shit with my neighbors on both sides of me, both older white guys. It was the type of shit I probably wouldn't have gotten into if I were white.

One guy was married to a younger woman, and I'd heard he felt insecure about that and didn't like seeing me and my friends. This is hearsay but it's pretty classic: a white guy who feels sexually threatened by Black guys. We'd sometimes hang out with our shirts off, and I heard he'd been grumbling to people about that. One time, my half brother was in the driveway washing my car and playing music, and my neighbor came out all pissed off and turned the radio off. The Black guy playing music too loud is a classic racial trope too.

The guy to the other side of me was always complaining about *something*: the lights were on in my driveway. The TV was *too loud*. We were talking *too loud*. Again, classic shit white people are always saying about Black people.

Another time, I had some people over and he complained, and I flipped out: *Lemme ask you something, motherfucker: Do you put a glass to the fucking door? It's always something with your ass. I'm sick of this shit.*

The condo association also had it out for me. There was a little island in my cul-de-sac where people could park, but at a certain point, they made it a fire zone, which eliminated the parking: I'm pretty sure this was done so I couldn't have people over.

Then, they sent me a letter that said if I was gonna have more than two people over, it would be considered a party and I'd have to notify the association.

After that, I knew my days there were numbered. I saw a place in Calabasas and fell in love with it. It's built into a side of a hill, six bedrooms, on a 3.5-acre property, with plenty of room for guests. I was an L.A. guy and here was my L.A. dream house. It was fifty-five miles from the Rams' facility, and with L.A. traffic, sometimes it took me two and a half hours to get to practice. But it was worth it, because it was where I felt I belonged.

◆

L.A., man. The feeling I always come back to is that I felt *free*. I was young, rich, and successful, a star in a town that runs on star power. Imagine being born in the segregated South, raised on a dirt road, and you wake up a few short years later and you're in a city that seems like it was tailor made for you.

The women, especially. I remember the female attention I got when I first got out here, how easy it all was, and thinking, *Damn! They all like brothers out here?!*

In L.A., at least in the circles I ran in, it wasn't about color. It was about *status*. I was twenty-three and I had that. I was dating more women than I could handle—literally. One year, I got Christmas gifts for six different women, and I spent all this time wrapping the gifts. Then I realized I'd forgotten to put their names on the wrapping paper, so I had to unwrap the gifts and start again.

Image was everything. Guys would go to the club in rented Ferraris to make it seem like they had money. When rap got big, all of a sudden half the Black guys in the club said they were rappers. Or football players. I don't know how many times a woman told me that so-and-so guy plays for the Rams, and I'd look over and wouldn't recognize him. Then, after *Coming to America* came out, every Black guy was shooting a movie. It was insane.

But I didn't have to lie. Just as it was on the football field, those first couple years, everything was too easy. It felt like one of those dreams I didn't want to end. I had to pinch myself to make sure it was real: I went on *Soul Train*. I went to the Oscars. Then my PR agency roped me into posing for *Playgirl*.

I was meeting all kinds of celebrities. It didn't quite occur to me that I was also a celebrity. One time I went to a party at the Playboy Mansion and hung out with Jack Nicholson, O. J. Simpson, and Pam Grier. I thought to myself: *I'm living in TV world. This isn't supposed to happen in real life.*

In '84, I was at an Italian spot on the Sunset Strip called Nicky Blair's, and Nicky, the owner, came over and said Clint Eastwood was there—and that he wanted to meet me. I'd grown up idolizing him: I loved how cool and gritty he was. That he didn't say much, but when he did, he was powerful and sarcastic. I wanted to be cool like that too. And here he was, wanting to meet *me*.

—*I'm a big fan, son,* he told me.

—*I'm a big fan too.*

We talked for a minute and he was real cool.

Another surreal moment: I saw Pam Grier at Carlos'n Charlie's—

and then I found out she was into me. Pam Grier! Ms. Foxy Brown herself! It was every Black man's dream. One thing led to another, and during training camp one year, we went back to my place and were making out. But then I checked the time, and I realized I had to be back at Cal State Fullerton for bed check, so we took a rain check and I drove back. After that, we fell out of touch, and I've regretted it ever since. Cockblocked by the curfew.

Carlos'n Charlie's was where all the Black celebrities hung out. I met Prince there: I was surprised at how tiny and shy he was, but he had a really strong handshake that stunned me. I met Denzel Washington when he was up and coming. Chaka Khan. Rick James.

Rick was the life of the party. That *Chappelle's Show* "I'm Rick James, bitch!" bit is *exactly* how he was. He was the man: loud, funny, the guy everyone wanted to be around. He loved football, so he and I became friends. He even put my name in the acknowledgments of one of his albums. Rick introduced me to my daughter's mother: that's a complicated situation I'll get into more later, but if it wasn't for Rick, my daughter wouldn't be around, so I have him to thank for that.

Mike Tyson. I met him in '87, back when he was on top of the world and back before I got shipped out to Indianapolis. I was at Nicky Blair's: Nicky said someone wanted to buy me a bottle of champagne, and I met Mike and we exchanged numbers. Then, a few weeks later, after I'd been traded, I ran into him at a party in New York. I can't remember why, but we found ourselves in an alley. He goes, *Here, lemme show you something*, and he puts up his hands and starts shadowboxing with me, flipping these punches to either side of my head. I'm telling you: those were the hardest, fastest punches I've ever seen, by far. I was trying to concentrate on not moving, because one small move to either side and he would've knocked me out.

—*Mike, Mike. Come on,* I told him, but he was still buzzing my ears left and right.

—*Mike. Don't knock me out in this alley here. Mike. Mike, come on, man.*

Finally he stopped. And I'm here to tell the tale.

•

My most cherished encounter with a celebrity? Muhammad Ali, easily.

Ali was *my guy* growing up. I idolized him. In my town, being an Ali guy *meant* something. The white people didn't like him, of course, and a lot of the Black people didn't either. Those "Mister Charlie's Boys," as we used to call them. The type of Black people who had the white man deep inside their heads, controlling every thought—and they were too ignorant to even know it. The guys who tripped over themselves with *Yes, sir!* every time the white man said something. The guys like the janitor at my school who told me I should obey my racist coach because he was a *good white man.*

Those guys hated Ali. They'd always call him a "loudmouth." And because they hated him, I loved him. The night he lost to Joe Frazier for the first time, I was ten years old and listened to it on the radio, and cried afterward.

I loved the pride he carried himself with. I loved how engaging he was with fans and kids, and that he treated people kindly, despite what the media said about him. I liked that he stood for what was right, and wasn't gonna let the white man run over him. I didn't know much about the Vietnam War when I was a kid, but I liked that he said he wasn't gonna go fight the white man's war. His famous line—*No Viet Cong ever called me nigger*—expressed something I felt. I was a young kid and didn't really follow politics, but in my bones, I couldn't understand why so many Black and poor people were being shipped off across the world to get killed.

I met him at an event after my rookie season, in Galveston, where I was being honored as Rookie of the Year and he was being honored for something else. People in the room *flocked* to him. As athletes, we're used to that, but this guy was different. Saying he had an *aura* is a cliché, but it's the best way I can describe it. I felt like I was ten again.

He was at the center of the crowd, but he also floated above it. You could tell he had a little shake from the Parkinson's, but it didn't take away from his presence. He had this wise, spiritual look in his eyes, like he knew the secrets of the universe but didn't have to explain them to the rest of us, because we wouldn't understand anyway. He was The Champ. The Greatest.

He looked at me. *You the football player?*

—*Yes, sir.*

—*You get women?*

That made me smile: *Yeah! I get a lot of women!*

—*You* don't *get women,* he said. *I get women.*

That cracked me up. He was showing me he was still The Champ.

About eight years later, I saw him in Denver at a promo event for some nutrition product. He looked a lot worse—the Parkinson's had progressed—but his mind was completely sharp and he was cool with me.

Then he did something I'll never forget. Something you won't believe when I tell you. But I don't care if you believe it or not: I saw it with my own two eyes.

He asked me: *You know the saying, "Float like a butterfly, sting like a bee?"*

I said yes.

Then he put his hands together and just stood there, like he was meditating. He closed his eyes. A moment later, his feet came off the ground, about three or four inches. It lasted for several seconds.

Muhammad Ali could tell the white man to fuck off. Muhammad Ali could also levitate.

And I'm not the only one who has seen this. A couple years later, I was talking to the wife of Ken Norton, the boxer. Kenny was my good friend, and he'd just gotten into a really bad car crash that left him compromised for the rest of his life. Kenny's wife Jackie told me that Ali had come to the hospital to visit Kenny—and had done the exact same thing.

◆

Those first few years in L.A. were a wild ride. It was fun, but it was a lot for a young kid to handle. That's what I was, really: a kid. People forget this because athletes are rich and famous. Maybe they also forget this because a lot of us are Black. But pro athletes are usually in their early to mid-twenties. They're kids.

That's why you see a lot of them blow through all their money. They're kids who came from nothing and are suddenly flush with cash. Kids who feel like they have to support their family and friends. Back then, the NFL provided absolutely no support structure, and it doesn't do nearly enough nowadays. I've always felt it was because the league, and much of the white general public, sees a bunch of Black guys losing their money and thinks it's because they're stupid.

But I was one of the lucky ones. I kept my money, for the most part, because I had a support structure: my mom. She was really smart about money and the way the world works. And because she was aware of how dangerous football is, she knew I could lose my paycheck any day.

She'd tell me, repeatedly: *Don't be paying for everyone. Don't be doing things for people. Don't do that, Eric. The money's gonna run out.*

She pounded that into me, which is good, because this isn't something you'd intuitively know when you're twenty-three and getting game checks for money you'd never dreamed of before. That money seems impossible to spend. It isn't.

People were constantly clawing at me. My stepdad—or, my biological mom's dad—needed a "loan" for his dump truck for his construction business. I helped him out, but of course I never saw that money again. All kinds of cousins needed money for this or that "business venture." People would take me out to dinner—but I'd always wind up picking up the tab.

People back home didn't understand: they just saw the salary in the paper. They had no idea that taxes eat half of that. They had no idea how quickly it could go. But my mom did. She ran interference for me with the people back home, telling them *no* so I didn't have to.

The whole thing was tough, because of course I wanted to help people. Of course I felt conflicted about getting rich while the people I grew up around stayed poor. There's a survivor's guilt that comes with being a pro athlete. People make fun of the guys who lose all their money, and trot out all the racist stereotypes, but often these guys are just too soft-hearted.

So I mostly kept my money. Sure, I splurged on some things, and scratched the itch of being young and rich. I love Italian dress shoes, so I got myself a closet full of those. I got a mink coat. I got some other nice clothes: I'd go to the club in a black leather jacket with black leather pants and a turtleneck, looking like Shaft. I got some cars, too: a Benz, a Porsche the Rams actually bought me for being Rookie of the Year, and then, later, a white Ferrari Testarossa I'd seen on *Miami Vice*.

And then, of course, came the biggest expense: my daughter Erica, who was born in 1987, and who was the best thing that ever happened to me, though I didn't realize it at the time. (I'll talk much more about my amazing daughter later.)

Also, my mom. She was gonna be taken care of. You have to understand: she raised me, so my success *was* her success. The things I got her weren't *gifts*. They were things that she herself had earned.

My rookie year, I made her quit her job cleaning houses on the white side of Sealy. While I was leading the league in rushing, my nearly eighty-year-old mom was saying *Yes ma'am, No ma'am* to a white lady forty years younger than her. That wasn't gonna fly. But I had to twist my mom's arm: she took pride in being a hard worker and she never, ever wanted to feel dependent on anyone.

I also bought her a Cadillac Coupe de Ville: red with a white top. I gave it to her for her birthday and had a big bow put on it. It still makes me smile to think about her face when she saw it.

Then I built her a house. That was very meaningful to me; I wasn't gonna let her keep living in a shotgun shack. I remember as a kid knowing how smart my mom was, and how hardworking she was, and wondering why she couldn't live in a nice house like the white people. So I built her a 2,800-square-foot Tudor, with four bedrooms.

The realtors wanted her to move to Westview, the white part of town, but she wasn't having that. So we built the house on the property she'd lived on for years, where I'd grown up. Our old house was on stilts, so we just moved it to the back of the lot, and a classmate of mine later bought it and moved it again. They later named the street after me, so the address of my mom's house became 518 Dickerson Street. I still own that house and go back at least once a year to visit.

At the time, she said to me, *I'm an old lady—why are you getting me this?* But she lived until 2000, so she lived in that house for a long time.

I paid that house off in one day. Just wrote a check. When you've never had money, when you've seen your mom work her ass off to feed you and clothe you, that's an incredible feeling.

The day after I paid the house off, I called my mom: *Mama, how'd you sleep last night?*

—*Best sleep I've ever had.*

CHAPTER 11

ERIC THE INGRATE

I don't remember the hit, but I remember lying on the field. I couldn't get up. I couldn't even move a limb.

Then I was in a wheelchair. People would visit me with sad, pitying looks on their faces. One minute, they'd wanted to be like me. Now they felt sorry for me.

It was the most terrifying dream I'd ever had. I think it was my junior year of college when I had it. Ever since I started playing football, I'd been afraid of getting paralyzed on the field. But that dream made the fear worse. After that, the fear popped into my head every couple of months. As the years went by, it took more and more effort to push it to the back of my mind.

I once told a writer from *Sports Illustrated* that football isn't a game, it's a business. Scrabble is a game, I told him, because you can't break your neck playing Scrabble. In football, it only takes one play. Every week, you'll see that guy writhing on the ground whose career—or even life—is never gonna be the same. As a player, it's not a question of *whether* that's gonna be you one day. It's only a question of *when* it's gonna happen, and how bad it's gonna be.

Before it did happen, I wanted to make some real money. Under my current contract, negotiated by an agent I later fired, that wasn't happening.

The contract was for four years and $2 million, but $600,000 of that was actually a forgivable loan. After I got traded, the Rams decided not to forgive it, and I had to give it back. For the first two years in the league, I was in the low six figures at a time when the top backs were getting close to a million per year. That's not a *team-friendly deal*. That's robbery.

By the end of the '84 season, my outlook about being a pro football player had begun to change. I was waking up to the way the league worked, no longer a wide-eyed rookie who was just happy to be there. The newspapers had started publishing players' salaries, and I'd see what other guys were making compared to my salary. I'd see how the Rams treated their players. Like how they'd cut guys who got injured in the middle of the season. Like how team leaders and good players would get traded, because while it's all about the team inside the locker room, it's all about profit for the people upstairs.

And as much as I loved L.A. and my teammates, the organization was a different story. With Georgia Frontiere as owner, we all had the sense that the organization didn't care if we won or not and that the focus was on protecting the owners' money. For years, we were a playoff team—but the organization didn't do the things, like get a good quarterback, that would've put us over the top. I had no problem with Georgia personally—she always struck me as a nice lady, and she and my mom got along—but playing for the Rams, I could clearly see that things were being done on the cheap and that we weren't a first-class organization.

For example, our practice facility was a junior high school in Orange County, with a shabby field and showers that were way too low, so you had to duck your head to get it wet. Our meeting room was a cramped classroom at the school with not enough desks, so some guys had to stand. The desks were the small ones with the wooden top you'd lift up. It was ridiculous to watch 250-pound elite athletes cram into desks that thirteen-year-olds used to learn algebra.

Another thing that was weird: we'd get two different game checks, from different banks. Years later, I ran into a guy who said he was the Rams' banker and we got to talking about it, and everything he said validated my impressions about the organization. He said the Rams were always cash poor, and were always moving money around to balance the books. He also told me that when the Rams traded for Jim Everett and gave him his signing bonus, Jim's check bounced.

After hearing that, it all made sense. I might not have known those details at the time, but what I did know was that I was playing for a second-class organization.

My rookie year, Georgia paid for an interior designer to decorate my apartment in Irvine, with modern artwork, a zebra-skin rug, and a king-sized bed with a velour headboard. It was nice of her, but after years of being underpaid, I came to think of it as a poor substitute for a fair contract. Because, shit, I can decorate my own apartment. (Related to this, Adidas, my shoe sponsor, got me a *cake* for breaking the rushing record. A *cake*. Except I couldn't even eat it because it was a carrot cake and I'm allergic to nuts.)

Being in the same city as the Lakers and Dodgers underscored that the Rams were just not on par. Both the Dodgers and Lakers were premier organizations that won multiple titles in the '80s, and their owners were beloved icons in L.A.. With Lakers owner Dr. Jerry Buss in particular, you could see the fondness he had for his players. Seeing the Lakers winning titles, and watching those guys make so much money and become big stars in L.A., made me a little envious that I was stuck out in Orange County with an organization that cut corners. We had a near-championship team and could've been on the level of those organizations if only management were more committed.

Some of the veteran Rams used to talk fondly about the previous owner, Carroll Rosenbloom, Georgia's husband, who'd died in 1979. Guys revered Carroll and said he genuinely cared about his players as people. To them, he was like Dr. Jerry Buss before Dr. Buss came on the scene. I heard that all the time in the locker room: *If Carroll were here* . . . But Carroll wasn't walking through that door.

As much as I loved the guys in the locker room, I found myself fantasizing about going to the 49ers or Washington, two organizations with reputations of taking care of their players. My cousin Dexter

Manley was a star with Washington, and we'd compare notes when we'd hang out in Texas in the offseason, and our feelings about our organizations couldn't have been more different.

All of it—my fear of injury, my feeling of having been ripped off my first two years in the league, the realization that the NFL is a business—was on my mind when I decided to hold out before the 1985 season.

◆

I wanted $1.4 million a season, but I was slated to get less than a third of that, which put me way, way down on the list of running backs. The Rams didn't budge. So I went back home to my mom's house when training camp started. I expected to be back in camp in just a few days, but then a week went by without a new deal, and then two weeks went by.

I wound up staying home for forty-seven days.

I was back in sleepy Sealy, laying low—it was almost like it was hiding out. I was bored as hell. I'd work out at the high school and at a gym, and rent movies and watch them all day. *A Fistful of Dollars, Hang 'Em High, For a Few Dollars More.* I *binged* those Clint Eastwood movies before the term "binge-watch" existed. This was before I'd built my mom her house, so I was in my small childhood house, and it didn't feel real that I'd met Eastwood the year before in glamorous L.A. Being back in Sealy, I was a long way from that world.

Sometimes I'd take my mom out to dinner; mostly she'd cook. She liked having me home because she was always worried I'd hurt myself playing football.

—*I hate that sport*, she'd say. *I hate that you're showing them your talent and they're not appreciating it.*

When I did venture out, a lot of people in Sealy gave me a hard time. It was the same people who had always been jealous of me, the type of people who get threatened when someone has the audacity to leave their small world and show how small it really is.

—Why you ain't at camp! they'd say. *You signed a contract!*

I got tired of having to explain that in the NFL, that logic doesn't hold. If I'd have gotten hurt and never played again, the Rams could've torn up my contract just like that. Shouldn't that go both ways?

But people didn't get it. In the '80s, when salaries for athletes started to explode, most fans couldn't understand how someone making multiple times what they made could possibly complain. They didn't get that if you were getting paid hundreds of thousands of dollars— more money than all but a handful of people in Sealy had ever seen— but producing $1.5 million in value, it's possible to be grateful for the money you're getting while still feeling like you're having a million dollars ripped out of your pocket. I couldn't explain to them that after two years of breaking records on an unfair deal, you start to become less grateful and more bitter.

While I sat at home, the sportswriters back in L.A. teed off on me. Our relationship had always been tense. I'd been mistrustful of the media since high school and had never been the warm and cuddly superstar they'd wanted. A lot of guys, many who come from rough home lives, seek validation from the media and love from the public, but that was never me. I got plenty of love at home from my mom and dad, so I didn't come to the media needing anything, and I think that rubbed people the wrong way. When I held out, the writers showed their true feelings about me.

The names they called me sting to this day: *Eric the Ingrate.* That word: *ingrate.* It even *sounds* like the N-word. It tells me I should be happy I was getting paid at all. It tells me to shut up and run.

They said I was a *locker room lawyer.* A *malcontent. Difficult, petulant*—basically any word they could think of as a substitute for *uppity.* That I was *not a team player,* because I was *all about the money.* The audacity I had to want to be paid *like a quarterback,* which, given the lack of Black quarterbacks, read to me like a coded way of saying that I wanted to get paid *like a white player.* (On that topic, when was the last time you saw a quarterback have to hold out to get what they deserve?)

The media instinctively takes the side of ownership in disputes with players, and back then it was even worse.

This is true for a couple of reasons: First, players are only with a franchise for a few years—really, we're just visiting—but ownership and the media are there for the long haul, so their perspective is the same. Second, NFL players are mostly Black, while ownership and the media are basically white institutions. That was even more true back when I played, when the writers in the Rams' locker room after a game were all white. So, yes, I'm saying that racism plays a huge role in how these things are covered, and that was even more the case back then.

Nowadays, we hear a lot of talk about *unconscious bias*, the way, as my mom would say, *it's just different for us.* When it comes to the way the media covered me, I got my first taste of this in high school, with the whole Trans Am thing, where I was made out to be some kind of criminal. Then, in college, when I struggled my first year, I was shocked by how vicious the writers were, and how gleeful they were that Craig James was doing better than I was. I was a teenage kid, and there were middle-aged columnists in a major American city arguing that they should take away my scholarship. Even at that age, I realized there was something fucked up about that, something dehumanizing. I knew there was no chance any of those columnists would want the same thing written about their teenage sons.

Then there was my holdout with the Rams. The writers were too savvy to say so explicitly, but they were basically trading on that old stereotype to describe me: *the angry Black guy.* It became a self-fulfilling prophecy, because after they wrote that shit, I became what they said I was.

To a large degree, that's been my reputation ever since. It's complete bullshit. Ask my teammates or anyone who knows me: my parents raised a standup guy and a loyal friend. They raised a guy who played as hard as anyone—and took a lot more punishment than most. Back then and even now, people tell me I'm nothing like how the media portrayed me. I never complained about my contract to teammates. When my teammates brought that stuff up to me, they'd say,

Man, Eric, we understand—but they're not paying me anything either. I responded that if management didn't pay me, they'd use that as leverage to not pay the other guys, which is exactly what they did.

All I did was ask for basic fairness, which is something every American should do. But yeah, *it's just different for us*, and for that, I was portrayed as a bad guy by a bunch of old white guys (the media) doing the bidding of another bunch of old white people (team management). The things they wrote were so unfair and made me feel so powerless. The best analogy I can think of is that it's like being convicted of a crime I didn't commit.

That was the writers. The fan mail I got didn't even bother with the coded language.

—*You niggers should play for free to entertain us.*

—*You're just a bunch of monkeys anyway.*

—*Why don't you go back to Africa.*

You get letters like that sent to your mom's house and it hurts, forever. Those letters remind you, as a Black person, that those people are out there, hiding in plain sight. They're the people waiting in line for your autograph. They're the people wearing your number 29 jersey. Those letters are the type of thing you can't unsee, the type of thing that forms your outlook for the rest of your life. If you've ever wondered why I've never been a cuddly superstar, why I'm not a Black guy who's easy for white people to embrace, look no further than those letters.

All of this stuff was stirred up in me again when Donald Trump as president attacked those NFL players for taking a knee to protest racial injustice. Real quick on Trump: he was an embarrassment, and still is. As the years pass, it's gonna seem more and more insane that he was our president. And for all his tough-guy talk, he's fucking soft, and pampered. He's never been punched in the mouth. He's never gone to bed hungry. He doesn't know what it's like to work a real job in the summertime in the heat. He knows nothing about toughness.

When he called those players sons of bitches, it was déjà vu for me. He was expressing the same idea as what you'd find in those newspaper columns and those letters: that if you're Black in this country and white people are paying you money, you don't have a right to your opinion. That if you're Black and you don't stay in line, you're an ungrateful nigger. That you were *given* an opportunity—as opposed to having *earned* it. That at the end of the day, the white man calls the shots.

This was the case when I played and it's still the case. Just look at Colin Kaepernick. I knew from the very beginning he'd get run out of the league and never play again. I said as much at the time on TV, on my regular spot as a football pundit on Fox Sports 1, and here we are all these years later.

His crime? Taking a knee. The most peaceful form of protest imaginable. Something he discussed ahead of time with a veteran to make sure it was respectful to the military.

I can't see how anyone could possibly disagree with what he was trying to point out. Yes, a lot of great things have been done in the name of that flag, but so have a lot of horrible things. Unjust wars. A legacy of white supremacy. Stealing land from the Native Americans and committing genocide. Stealing people from Africa and enslaving them. Kaepernick was trying to make people stop and reflect. But white America doesn't like reflecting on things that make it uncomfortable.

Think about what Kaepernick did and how pissed off people were about it. Now think about what those crazy Trump supporters did for their "protest" at the Capitol, and how they were basically allowed to just waltz right in and take selfies with the cops. Can you imagine what would've happened if thousands of Black people had rushed the Capitol? They would've brought out the military and they'd have been picking up bodies from the steps for weeks afterward. A lot of white people saw what happened at the Capitol and were shocked. Black people weren't.

That's what Kaepernick was getting at, and that's what the NFL didn't want to hear. When you're Black in America, all of society's machinery is stacked against you. In my case, that meant team ownership and the media. For all Black people, that means the police.

My mom drilled that into me when I was growing up: *Eric, you can't trust the police. If they pull you over, it's "Yes sir, no sir." The minute you make a wrong move, they'll shoot you. And when the police report comes out, they'll have a whole different story.*

I have a young son now. In a couple of years, I'll be telling him the same thing. Black people call it The Talk. Among us, it needs no further explanation. Everyone knows what it is.

After that cop murdered George Floyd, the NFL made a big thing about finally "getting it" and wanting to fight racism. Commissioner Roger Goodell and the league pledged to donate $250 million over ten years for anti-racism efforts. But that's chump change to them. They also wrote *END RACISM* in the end zones, which is a good marketing move but nothing more. Goodell publicly apologized to Kaepernick, but sometimes sorry doesn't cut it. Because Kaepernick is still out of the league. Because while the league is 70 percent Black, as of this writing there are only three Black head coaches and five Black general managers.

The NFL's messaging may have changed because it had to. But the underlying reality has not.

•

As the weeks went by in '85, being at home was taking its toll. All the stuff being said and written about me hurt, but so did the fact that I wasn't with my teammates. I was bereft. Every August since I started playing the sport, I'd been in training camp, and I came to love that smell in the air that told you football was coming. To smell that smell while stuck at my mom's house watching movies felt weird. My holdout dragged on, and the preseason games started, then the real games. Watching the sport go on without you is a terrible feeling for an athlete with pride.

Charles White, who I'd admired when he was at USC, did a nice job at running back in my place, and the Rams went 2–0. I was rooting for Charlie but with each passing day, holding out was becoming more and more intolerable. After Week 2, my agent at the time, Jack Rodri, presented me with a contract he said was fair. I knew in my heart that it wasn't, but I was desperate to get back and so was inclined to take his word for it. I signed the deal, which essentially paid me a $500,000 bonus to report back to the team, with the verbal promise that the Rams would negotiate a fair long-term deal with me.

I went back with mixed feelings. Despite the $500,000 bump, I was still horribly underpaid relative to my production. I was skeptical the Rams were sincere in their promise to work out a long-term deal, and I worried my agent—who'd been Ken Norton's agent, and took me as his first football client—was in over his head in dealing with the Rams general manager John Shaw, who was hated among the players but was undeniably smart. It turned out I was right about both things.

My first game back was in Seattle. The crowd in the Kingdome booed me *hard*. I'd known from my time in Sealy that the national media had written a lot about my holdout and that I'd become a pariah, and hearing those boos in Seattle, of all places, brought that fact home. Right then, a part of me realized the die had been cast on my reputation and that in the minds of football fans everywhere, I'd always be the *malcontent*, the *ingrate*. Holdouts at that time were much less common than they were just a few years later, and when I heard those boos in Seattle, I realized it wasn't just Rams fans who were offended. The whole NFL apparatus—ownership, media, and fans—couldn't abide the idea of a Black guy who advocated for himself without apology. A Black guy who wasn't "Mister Charlie's Boy."

Early in the game, on a third-down play, the Kingdome crowd got really loud, as Seattle crowds are now famous for. I got the ball and busted into the open field for a 43-yard run, and the crowd went silent. All you could hear was our sideline cheering. It was damn satisfying: if they wanted me to be the guy wearing the black hat, fine. Fuck them and fuck everyone. At that moment, it felt like it was me and my teammates against the world.

That day, we blew out the Seahawks and I rushed for 150 yards and 3 touchdowns. I'd only practiced for three days since returning from my holdout and I was *still* that good. *That* was what mattered, not what the writers wrote about me or what these people thought about me.

◆

But the 1985 season was tough. In that Seattle game, I broke my wrist, and all season long I had hamstring problems, which were probably related to the holdout. The Rams sent me to yoga classes, but I hated it and it never took. That season, after being out for forty-seven days, I always felt like I was clawing back from behind. Game after game, reporters would ask me the same question over and over, in so many words: *What's up with you?* They'd say it with an edge, an accusing tone, as if I'd done something to them personally.

Still, we put together an 11–5 season and won the division for the first time in my career, earning us a home playoff game against Dallas in the divisional playoffs. Which is when, after a regular season that had left a foul taste in my mouth, I had the best game of my career.

I went off for 248 yards. It's a playoff record that still stands. For one day, I could forget about the bullshit surrounding the business of the game. The game itself was enough—and the game was perfect.

Sixty degrees in Anaheim Stadium, one of those games where the field looks about 50 percent wider, like you could run for days. Every hole I chose was the right hole, every cut I made was the right cut. Every play we called was perfect for the defense they were playing. In every one-on-one situation with a defender, I'd either make him miss or run him over. Every play, it seemed, went for 8 yards, 12 yards, 15 yards.

Before one play, with our team up 13–0 with the ball on the Cowboys' 40, I took one look at the defense and just knew I was gonna score a touchdown. The play was a toss right to me, and everything broke exactly the way I knew it would: a seal block that cut off the defensive end, a kickout block, and there was the seam. I bucked a D-back who tried to tackle me high—in the open field I was too big and too fast— and I was off and flying.

Flying. That's what it felt like. Frictionless, everything smooth and quiet. There had been so much bullshit all year, but as long as there were moments like these, I would always love this game.

After the play, an NFL Films camera caught me telling David Hill, *I knew it was gonna be a touchdown.* I loved being so good at something that I could tell things were gonna happen before they happened. That game brought me back to the feeling I'd had my first two years in the league but hadn't felt all season: *I love this game so much, I'd play it for free.*

We routed the Cowboys 20–0 that day. That's my signature game, the first one the NFL has on YouTube when you punch in my name. All those people these days who like to question the value of running backs can go watch that game: in a game where we blew out the opponent, our quarterback, Dieter Brock, was 6 for 22, for 50 yards and 1 interception and a 20.6 rating.

After the game, a reporter asked John Robinson how he'd stop me if he were coaching the other team. *I'd have him hold out,* he joked.

We were off to the NFC Championship in Chicago. But there, all the good vibes from the previous week were wiped out. It was freezing and gray and miserable. The Bears stacked the box on us and dared Dieter to beat them, and Dieter wasn't up to the task. I had 46 yards on 17 carries and fumbled twice. The Bears were talking shit to me all game, and so were the fans, who were throwing stuff at us on the sideline. It was awful.

I also played most of that game with a concussion—something that didn't raise eyebrows back then but scares me in retrospect. I got it in the first quarter, on a 3rd-and-1 play, when Richard Dent caved in our side of the line and gave Mike Singletary a free run at me. I didn't see Singletary coming and he hit me with all he had, which was a lot, and when I got up from that play I saw two rainbows crossing into stars.

The trainer asked me, *You alright?* I said I was.

—*Where are you?*

—*Chicago.*

—*Who are you playing against?*

—*Bears.*

—*What's your name?*

—*Eric Dickerson.*

—What's your date of birth?

That I didn't know.

They told me I was alright, that it was just a "ding," that I should get back out there. In that era, you were expected to play through a "ding" for your organization. So I did.

◆

That was such a frustrating loss because that '85 Rams team was really, really good and had a legit shot of winning the Super Bowl. The team had all the elements—except a quarterback. And the organization's failure to get one was one of many ways it was cutting corners and taking the cheap way out.

The Rams hadn't had the same quarterback for two straight years since the '70s, and after the '84 season, we knew we desperately needed one. Our starter in '84 was Jeff Kemp, a nice guy, but the definition of a career backup, who passed for fewer yards than I rushed for that year.

With a team ready to compete for a Super Bowl, with one obvious hole, the organization brought in Dieter Brock—a thirty-four-year-old who'd played his entire career in Canada, and who nobody had ever heard of. Nothing against Dieter personally, but this pissed me off then and it pisses me off now. The Rams cheaped out of paying me, which took money out of my pocket. And they cheaped out of paying a quarterback, which helped waste my prime years.

Earlier I'd heard we were interested in Warren Moon. I don't know why this didn't happen—was it the money, or something else about Warren?—but think about how history would've changed if we'd have gotten that done. We would've had a Hall of Famer at running back in me, a Hall of Famer at quarterback in Warren, and a Hall of Famer at left tackle in Jackie and a bunch of other perennial Pro Bowlers on the line, and most of us would've been in our primes. If Warren was our quarterback, Henry Ellard—the best route runner I've ever seen, who at the time was more feared than Jerry Rice—would've been a sure-fire Hall of Famer as well. We would have had a historically talented offense.

Instead, we had Dieter, who played just one season in the NFL, during which we dragged him to the NFC Championship game but couldn't drag him any further. I don't want to be too hard on Dieter because I have nothing against the guy, but during those two playoff games, in the year that was my best shot at winning a Super Bowl, my quarterback was a combined 16 for 53, for 116 yards and 2 picks, and he fumbled twice.

We finally tried to address the quarterback position after the '86 draft by trading for Jim Everett, who the Oilers had just taken with the third overall pick. Jim had a strong arm and he was a big, tall guy, and it was obvious he had talent. That was the good news. The bad news for me was that the Rams were still crying poor and were making it clear they had no intention of reworking my contract like they'd promised—and Jim was making more money than me from the moment he came in. No knock on Jim, but he hadn't accomplished anything in the league and I was in the middle of the best prime a running back has ever had. Something was definitely wrong with that picture.

It was the accumulation of slights that slowly but surely took the fun out of the game for me after my first two years. It became a job. But that didn't mean I was any less committed to it or good at it. In '86, I was healthy again, and for the third time in my four years in the league, I led the league both in rushing and in yards from scrimmage.

Despite getting Jim, we had three different quarterbacks start at least five games, but still we went 10–6 and got into the playoffs. The best moment of the year was when we went into Soldier Field on a cold late-season night and beat the Bears, 20–17. It was basically the same Bears team and same Rams team as the year before. I never bought into the mystique of the '85 Bears and I knew we could go toe-to-toe with them, and that game showed them we were never scared of them. The year before, they had talked so much shit: their defensive coordinator, Buddy Ryan, said our linemen never got called for holding and that that was the only reason my numbers were so good. Safety Gary

Fencik implied that I'd been afraid of Mike Singletary, who'd gone to Baylor, since my college years. Well, fuck all that. It was nice to show those guys who we were: a physical football team that ran the ball down teams' throats, the Bears included.

We were 10–6 heading into the playoffs and I liked our chances. Our first-round game was on the road against Washington, and I liked the way our running game matched up against their defense.

It was a cold, overcast day and a late 4 p.m. start, and the crowd at RFK Stadium was impressive. The stands were a sea of burgundy. You could feel that East Coast intensity, where it felt like everyone in the D.C. region was packed into that stadium, practically on top of you, screaming. It was so different from our sparse crowds out in Orange County, where we were at a remove from all the energy of L.A.

The night before, I'd gone out to dinner with my cousin, Dexter Manley, who'd told me Washington had a bounty on me. Bounties were commonplace back then, and I bet they still are. The Saints Bountygate in 2009–2011 wasn't a scandal to anyone who has ever played an NFL game. We all know what a vicious sport this is, which is why I insisted on getting paid.

I wasn't afraid of Washington's bounty, but I went out and played the worst game of my entire career. We lost 19–7, and it was my fault. I fumbled on my second carry when we were driving into their territory—one of three fumbles I had in the game. That day, it felt like I was trying to hold onto a greased bottle. Fumbling gets in your head: when you have one fumble, all you can think of is, *Don't fumble again.* That day, after my second fumble, I felt like a liability out there. And then I fumbled *again.*

That was the game I got chased down from behind by Darrell Green, which everyone brings up like it was some humiliating thing. But I don't feel that way at all. It's football, and Darrell was the fastest guy ever to play the game, and he was faster than me.

What gets me about that game was that other than the fumbles, our running game was clicking: I had 158 yards on 26 carries. Play for play, we were the better team that day—we outgained them 324 to 228—except we had six turnovers and they had none. Cut out my fumbles from that game and we win. Those Rams teams in the mid-'80s were really special, and after that '86 playoff loss, I had a feeling our window was closed.

I was right. That game was the last time I'd ever get the chance to make a playoff run with those guys. I was heartbroken that I'd let them down.

◆

Coming into the '87 season, the writing was on the wall for me and the Rams. We were coming up on two seasons since my '85 holdout, and it was becoming more and more obvious the Rams had no intention of paying me.

That year was the strike year, but to be honest I was so focused on my own situation that I didn't pay much attention to the strike. Nowadays I feel bad about this: it was selfish of me, I realize in retrospect, because they were fighting for free agency and benefits for retired players. Guys would approach me wanting to talk about this stuff and I gave them an answer that satisfied them, but my heart wasn't in it. One thing I *wouldn't* do was throw shit at the bus the scabs took to the games. When you grow up in the South as a Black kid, that shit doesn't sit right. Either way, with my contract situation, nobody had to worry I'd cross the picket line.

That season was bad from the beginning. We started off 0–2 and then went on strike for three games, and by the time the strike was over, with the replacement players losing two of three, we were 1–4 and basically out of contention.

I can't remember exactly when in 1987, but I had been trying desperately to get a meeting with John Shaw, the Rams GM. I wanted to salvage the situation and I'd convinced myself that if I could just make my case personally, he might listen.

I'd never met Shaw but I'd heard plenty of bad things about him. Without a doubt, he was the most unpopular guy in the Rams' locker room. Players saw him as a bean counter and not a football guy, and he had this high, nasally voice that got on guys' nerves—probably because they only heard it from across the negotiating table when he was trying to screw them. Knowing what I know now about the Rams' finances, I don't blame Shaw entirely: it was his job to protect the owners' money while trying his best to put a winning team on the field. We saw him as a snake. He saw himself as a tough negotiator who had a job to do.

But he did himself no favors. Years later, I heard that he was fond of saying that football players are like horses: they can be as unhappy as they want to be, but once you open the gate, they're gonna run. At the time, I didn't know that that was his mantra, but the sentiment came across in the way all of us felt disrespected. The guy was comparing a bunch of young, Black men to animals. Now, I'm not accusing Shaw of being a racist, but that's an example of how in the NFL, casual racism is in the air we all breathe. And while you couldn't say something like that publicly today, you better believe most people running NFL franchises think that way.

For weeks, I tried to get that meeting with Shaw, but he kept pushing me off: *This week he can't do it, something came up,* etcetera. I couldn't believe I was being blown off like I was some intern. It said a lot about how much the Rams valued their players, and the politics of football, that the best player in franchise history couldn't get a meeting with the GM. Put it this way: imagine if LeBron James wanted to speak with the Lakers' GM but was denied a meeting.

After weeks of trying, I finally got my meeting and drove down to the Rams' offices in L.A., in a two-story brick building on Pico Boulevard. It was small and run-down, which surprised me at the time but in retrospect was consistent with everything I'd come to hear about the Rams' finances. I took a tiny elevator up to Shaw's office, which had one small window facing the parking lot.

I got right to the point: I want to play for the Rams, I told him, but my contract needed to be reworked. I asked for $1.5 million a season.

—*You've got two years on the contract you got.*

That's the standard line for management types in football and those who support them: *You signed a contract!* It's a bullshit line, for the obvious reason that these contracts aren't binding on both sides.

He also told me that even after four years in the league, I still had to prove myself.

I couldn't believe I'd just heard that, so I started rattling off my stats: I told him I'd led the league in rushing in each of my four years except the year I held out, that I'd just led the league in rushing the previous year.

—*No you didn't, Eric. Walter Payton did.*

I was fucking floored. We went back and forth a few times—*Yes I did; No you didn't*—until he said he'd go look it up, and he got up to get some stat book.

—*Ohhh, you diiid!!!* He said it in that high, nasal voice.

I wanted to fucking smack him. There was no way in hell he didn't know that I'd led the league in rushing the previous year. That was something even casual football fans knew. What he was doing was playing some weird power game. It was his way of showing me that whatever my accomplishments were, they weren't important enough for him to know about them.

Even after this, I still thought he'd be receptive to the offer I put to him: I told him that I was so confident in my ability that I'd accept a one-year contract under the same terms as Elway and Marino's long-term deals. Both guys were making about $1.5 million a year, about three times what I was. I told him that if in the next season I didn't lead the league in rushing, that we could revert back to the deal I was playing under now.

Shaw didn't budge.

—*But you're not a quarterback, Eric.*

I told him that the way our offense ran, in terms of the number of yards I was expected to produce, I basically *was* the quarterback of our team.

Truth be told, if Shaw would've offered $1 million for that season, I would've taken it. But he didn't move an inch. He kept saying that if he redid my contract, all the guys would ask for new contracts.

We went around in circles for the hour or so I was in there. At first, I'd held out hope that he'd say something like *Okay, we'll do this, just don't tell anyone.* But as the hour went on, it became obvious that wasn't gonna happen.

I left feeling completely dejected, convinced this wasn't gonna work out. The best comparison I can think of is that my time with the Rams was like dating a girl you're in love with, but there are certain things about her that make it fatally flawed, and the more you try to make it work, the more you realize there's stuff you just can't get past.

Everything went downhill fast after my meeting with Shaw. I heard from people in the know that the Rams were shopping me. After that, I went into the office of Jack Faulkner, the pro personnel director, and asked him straight up if any teams were looking to trade for me. He looked me in the eye and said no, and I knew for a fact he was lying. At that point, I knew I couldn't trust anybody.

•

The last domino to fall was my relationship with John Robinson, and the way that ended makes me sad still.

The first game back from the strike, we played the Cleveland Browns on Monday Night Football, and I had a bad thigh bruise. We were 1–4 and I felt as disdainful about the organization as I'd ever felt. My meetings with Shaw and Faulkner were fresh in my mind. Under other circumstances, I would have played. But playing would've been going above and beyond the call of duty for an organization that had disrespected me.

I told John my thigh was really hurting me, and that I was gonna sit out against Cleveland. He told me that if I didn't play, he was gonna suspend me.

I can still see him telling me that, and I remember how awful it made me feel. It hurts me still.

I loved John from the moment I showed up at Rams training camp.

He was charismatic, he was funny, he was warm, he was approachable. He'd do tiddlywinks and horseshoes tournaments at practice. He was a genuinely kind, good human being. He was a father figure to me and also a friend. The season before, in our emotional Monday night win against the Bears, I had carried the ball about thirty times and took a beating. We flew straight to New Orleans for the next week's game, and John came up to me in the back of the plane and asked me, *Can you do it again?* And the way he looked at me, on top of how well he'd always treated me, showed me that he appreciated what I did for this team. It showed me that he thought of me as more than just a piece on a chess board. It showed me he genuinely cared about me. I told him yes, I could do it again, because throughout my Rams career I would have run through a brick wall for that man.

My mom would always say to me, *Eric, you got a fault: that loyalty of yours. You're gonna realize everyone's not as loyal as you.*

I realized it when John threatened to suspend me. It felt like the ultimate betrayal. The whole time, all I'd wanted him to do was come out publicly on my side and say, *Get him paid.* But that had never happened.

Looking back, I understand that John was caught in office politics. It was his job to stand between his players and the organization, and he was in a terrible position. I understand it and I forgive him—but I haven't forgotten. You don't forget that kind of hurt.

After that conversation with John, I was convinced that nobody had my back in the organization. I told the writers that week that since John got paid more than I did, maybe *he* should run 47 Gap. The writers treated the comment like the rantings of the Angry Black Man who was at it again. They wrote about it as if I'd burned the bridge with the Rams once and for all. What they didn't realize was that the Rams had already burned the bridge with me.

Against Cleveland, in that Monday night game, Charles White started. I dressed but sat on the bench. I hated not being there for my teammates, but that feeling only goes so far. We fell behind 20–0 and Charlie was getting beaten up out there. In the second quarter, he got injured, and I had to go in. I was so mentally checked out that I couldn't find my helmet. Finally I found it, and on the first play I got tackled in the backfield and the Cleveland crowd went crazy. Just like I'd been in Seattle in '85, I was a villain throughout the league, the face of all the *ingrates* out there.

A few plays went by. I couldn't get in the flow and had no desire whatsoever to be out there. And then I broke a 27-yard touchdown run.

After that play I told the coaching staff my thigh hurt, that I needed to come out of the game. It was my last play in a Rams uniform.

◆

Fast-forward a few days. I hadn't spoken to John Robinson all week. It was Halloween night. I was at my house in Calabasas about to head over to a party in Hollywood, and Jim Gray was over at my place. Yes, *that* Jim Gray, the famous reporter, who was an up-and-comer back then and always gave me a fair shake. We're still friends.

That night, I was wearing a costume that would probably get me in trouble today: I was an Indian chief, with a big headdress, buckskin pants, moccasins, a tomahawk, and face paint. I grew up in Texas watching cowboys-and-Indians movies, and *I always rooted for the Indians*. Ever since I was a kid, my mentality was to stick it to The Man.

The phone rang. Jim wanted me to ignore it, but I figured I'd just pick it up. I heard an enthusiastic, gravelly voice on the other end.

—*Hey, Big E!*

I recognized that voice: it was Ron Meyer. I loved Coach Meyer— but I hadn't thought about him in years.

—*Coach?*

—*Wanna come play for me?*

I had no idea he was the head coach of the Indianapolis Colts until he told me. He told me he'd just traded for me and that he'd worked out the numbers to get me the contract I'd been asking for: I'd be getting $1.5 million a year for the next four years. I flashed back in my mind to when Ron came to my shotgun house on that dirt road in Sealy. He had his gold, diamond-encrusted Concord watch and his Super Bowl ring. He told me he'd make me a millionaire one day. I hadn't forgotten that, and neither had he.

—*Didn't I tell you I'd make you rich one day?*

Ron's voice could get you excited about anything. Including $1.5 million a year, no doubt.

He told me to go to the airport, and catch the 12:30 red-eye flight from John Wayne to Indianapolis.

—*We're playing the Jets this weekend!*

The next few hours were surreal. Mixed, intense emotions. I was excited about playing for Coach Meyer, and about my money. I was in shock that the Rams had traded me. People underestimate the emotional impact of being traded, especially for a young player. I needed to get away from the Rams, but the trade still felt like a painful rejection.

I mumbled something to Jim Gray about the trade. He was as shocked as I was. Before I caught my flight, he wanted to do an interview with me, so we hopped in the car and headed to his network's studio. I was driving fast, and, to make a weird night even weirder, I got pulled over.

I told the cop who I was, and that I'd just been traded. He was shocked too, and he let me go. Then Jim and I did the interview and I caught my flight to Indianapolis.

CHAPTER 12

TO SIBERIA

The first doubts hit me on the red-eye.

After the plane took off, I looked out the window and saw the lights from the L.A. area stretch on and on, and on and on, until eventually there was just darkness.

Then I fell asleep. When I woke up, it was morning, and I looked out my window and saw nothing but cornfields. Right then, I realized how much my life had just changed.

I later learned that in the previous few weeks, as the idea of trading me was becoming inevitable, John Shaw had been saying, *I'm gonna send him to Siberia.* Seeing those cornfields out the window, that's exactly how it felt.

I'd wanted to get traded to Washington, so I could play with my cousin, Dexter Manley, who thought the world of Joe Gibbs and the way the organization treated its players. San Francisco was another place I would've loved to go to, especially with Bill Walsh's offense. Practicing in just helmets and shorts with no hitting. A Hall of Fame quarterback. Winning Super Bowls.

But this was 1987, before free agency. Players had no right to self-determination. You went where they told you to go.

I knew nothing about Indiana or the Colts. I didn't remember that was the franchise John Elway didn't want to play for after the '83 draft. I didn't know Bob Irsay was a mean, racist drunk.

At my first press conference, reporters asked me if I could convert Indianapolis from a basketball town to a football town. But I didn't know anything about that and hadn't seen *Hoosiers*. They also asked me about Bobby Knight, and I didn't know anything about him—but if I knew there was a guy who became a legend by screaming at Black kids who weren't getting paid, I wouldn't have liked him. In those few days and weeks after the trade, I didn't know anything. The only thing going through my mind was, *How in the hell did I end up here?*

By sticking up for myself with the Rams, I knew I'd done the right thing. But was this the right *place?*

Early signs pointed to no. During one of my first practices, it was bitter cold. I'd never experienced anything like it in Texas or L.A.

I sidled over to Ron and said, *It's too damn cold for me.*

He laughed and took it easy on me. He told me to make up a bullshit excuse that my hamstring was tight so I could go back inside the facility. But he said I'd have to get used to the weather soon enough.

There's no simple way to describe my time in Indianapolis, because it was a mixed bag just like anything. I have fond memories and bitter ones. I made a lot of great friends but met a lot of bad people. I played with guys who wanted to win and dogs who just wanted to cash their checks. But from the very beginning, I just knew it wasn't the place for me.

It hurt me that the situation with the Rams didn't work out because I loved L.A. and I loved my teammates. I knew that if I was a white guy who'd set an NFL record, there's no chance in hell they would have traded me or made me pay back most of my signing bonus. That bothers me to this day: I set records for that franchise for way, way below market value, and they chose not to forgive that loan? That's low-class.

I didn't miss the organization, but I missed my old life. Everything about Indy seemed small-time to me after coming from L.A. I missed the nightlife. I missed the weather. I kept my house in L.A. and would go back whenever I could during the season, and I lived there in the offseason. It was home and would always remain home. At night, I'd literally dream that I was still playing for the Rams. When I woke up to reality, I was always disappointed.

Playing in the Hoosier Dome was another part of the experience that made me feel dislocated. It was just . . . *weird*. Because I was coming from the sunny skies of Southern California, it felt like playing inside the Michelin Man. You had no idea what the weather was like outside. We'd have a 1 p.m. game, and after the game we'd walk outside and it was still light out. That got me, every time. John Shaw had said he wanted to send me to Siberia, but playing in the Hoosier Dome felt like playing on the moon.

◆

But there were some positives to my time in Indy, especially early on. My first year there, '87, was a fun season: we made the playoffs for the first time since the team moved to Indianapolis, and it was cool to see the excitement in the city build up. Ron was always fun to play for, and it was rewarding being a part of that with him. We'd won a lot at the college level; now, years later and both of us much richer, we were doing it in the pros.

There wasn't much to do in Indy, so I spent most of my free time chasing women and fucking. That's no exaggeration. Sex was just a huge part of what I thought about when I wasn't in practice: Which women are gonna show up that night to the Safari Bar, the spot in town all the Pacers and Colts went to?

On first blush, the women in Indianapolis were those corn-fed, wholesome ones. But really, they were freaks dying to get out. I had been in L.A., where the sex was in the air, but I swear, the freakiest shit I ever saw, or did, was in Indy: The first time that two women had sex right in front of me. The first (and only) time a woman drove to my house butt-naked, just in heels, had sex with me, and then drove back home.

Those Midwestern white women were into the brothers. I can't tell you how many times I heard, *I'm from Brownsburg*—the lily-white suburb—*I've never had a Black guy before*. But that's the way it was:

these women were cooped up and wanted to be wild, and in Indiana in the '80s, getting with a brother was wild. And since things were so boring for everyone there, all the freaky shit was ratcheted up. The women were crazy about athletes too, because unlike in L.A., sports were the only big-time thing in town.

I was still in my twenties, so my sex drive hadn't slowed down at all. A part of me is grateful social media and dating apps weren't around when I played. Sex was too easy back then, but talking to current players, I've heard it's about a hundred times easier now. I think I would've fucked myself to death.

Maybe literally. Because in that era, even though AIDS was spreading fast, it just wasn't something I thought about. In my mind, AIDS was just something that wasn't gonna happen to me, and it was the same for everyone I hung around. Sometimes I wore a rubber, sometimes I didn't. Either way, I didn't think much about it.

And then, in 1991, Magic Johnson announced to the world that he had HIV, and that shook me to my core. It was shattering: I felt awful for Magic and terrified for myself, especially because I knew Magic and I had slept with some of the same women. A few weeks after the announcement, for insurance reasons I needed to take a physical that required an AIDS test, and I was scared to death in the days leading up to it. Back then, before antiretroviral drugs, we all thought Magic would waste away and die in the next couple of years. Would I be next?

I was negative. I got lucky. Too many other people didn't.

•

In my last couple years in Indianapolis, I had some problems with some offensive linemen who simply weren't trying hard enough on the field, and I'll get into that later. But even though the Colts weren't nearly the type of close-knit team the Rams had been, I made some really good friends there.

The guy I hung out with most was Fredd Young, a linebacker the Colts traded for in '88 after he made a few Pro Bowls with the Seahawks. Fredd's calling card was special teams. The guy was just a guided missile on kickoffs, and as a Seahawk, he'd once laid out the Raiders' returner on one of those clips the NFL used to show all the time before they started pretending they cared about player safety.

Fredd was a good dude, a Texas guy like me, a guy who chased women as hard as I did: if you saw me at the Safari Bar, you saw him. I wasn't much of a drinker, but Fredd was one of those shy guys who needed a little alcohol to loosen him up. Once he had a couple drinks in him, he'd unleash his Latin-lover alter ego, *Fredduardo,* the name he'd use to introduce himself to women at clubs. He was a light-skinned Black guy with blue eyes, so he was playing up his distinctive look.

There were other good guys, too many to list. Harvey Armstrong, a defensive lineman who grew up in Houston, was someone I respected ever since he hosted me on my SMU recruiting trip. He was a vocal leader in the locker room who left it all out there on the field. Harvey was drafted in the seventh round and scratched out eight years in the league—and it wasn't until his seventh year that he became a full-time starter. He was a hard worker who took pride in his effort and cared about winning above all else.

Jeff Herrod was another good friend of mine. He'd been a ninth-round draft pick out of Ole Miss, and he worked his ass off to become a premier inside linebacker, even if he never quite got the credit. The guy went full speed in practice all the time and was a beast in the weight room: he was one of those no-neck guys who could bench 450 pounds.

He was proud of being Black, and I used to give him shit about going to Ole Miss: *What is your Black ass doing running with a rebel flag in your hand?*

Jeff's wife was a sister who hated all of us for messing with white women. Even light-skinned Black women couldn't escape her wrath. Jeff used to give me a hard time too, but I'd kid him: *One day, you're gonna get with a white woman.* Funny how life works: he wound up divorcing his wife, marrying a white woman, and having two kids with her. Prejudice is dumb, in either direction.

I didn't get along with some of my offensive linemen, but some others I liked a lot. Randy Dixon was a quiet, blue-collar guy who got the most out of his talent.

Brian Baldinger was the toughest guy I'd ever played with. You never wanted to start a fight with Baldy unless you were prepared to finish it. I once saw him get into it with a defensive player in practice: Baldy pulled the guy's facemask clear off his helmet and started hitting him with it. We needed more tough guys like that on our O-line.

Chris Hinton was a good guy and an athletic freak: we'd call him the "Dancing Bear." After going months of not working out, Chris could go into the weight room and throw up 400 pounds six or seven times, then go dunk a basketball. He was quiet and reserved—except when he drank, and then he'd get rambunctious.

Eugene Daniel was Mr. Colt: he was drafted in the eighth round and played thirteen years in the league, twelve of them with the Colts. He studied his ass off, worked out hard, and didn't get into trouble. He was an example of what it takes to have a long career.

Clarence Verdin was a trip: a little, funny, very knowledgeable guy. He knew everything about current events and could talk about any subject, so we called him CNN.

Those were some of my teammates who were bright spots during my time in Indy. And then, outside the organization, then there was Uncle Jimmy.

Uncle Jimmy was a distant cousin of mine, but for some reason everyone called him Uncle Jimmy, and I did too. He was a mysterious guy like that, a true gangster who ran "ticket houses" for running numbers in Indianapolis. He was from Texas originally and I have no clue how he got to Indianapolis, but there was a lot I didn't know about Uncle Jimmy. The one thing I and everyone else knew about him was this: you didn't fuck with Uncle Jimmy. You fucked with him, you ended up dead.

Uncle Jimmy once got robbed by two guys, and during the robbery, one of the guys shot Jimmy . . . but didn't kill him. That was a bad move on that guy's part. Later, those two guys were found burned in the trunk of a car.

For me, Uncle Jimmy was a good guy to know. We had played Cleveland in a Monday game in 1988, and when I came back afterward in the early morning hours, I discovered my apartment had been robbed: my jewelry and gun were gone. Cash, new clothes, jackets, bracelet, a diamond ring—all gone. It was freezing that night and I was exhausted, but I had to call the cops and deal with them and file a report, even though it seemed unlikely they'd make the situation right for me.

The next day, I called Uncle Jimmy.

—*I'll find out who did that shit, he told me.*

The next day, I saw Jimmy.

—*I got a lead on who did that shit.*

A few days later, Jimmy had gotten all my stuff back. I have no idea how. With Uncle Jimmy, you didn't ask questions.

—*I'll make sure that shit don't happen ever again,* he told me, and that was that.

Since my playing days, I've made a point of introducing guys that come through Indy to Uncle Jimmy. He and Marshall Faulk became great friends, for instance.

But while Uncle Jimmy knew the angles, he didn't know everything: he used to keep money in the floorboards of his house, $100,000 in cash, and one time during a heavy rainstorm, the money got wet. In an attempt to dry it off, he put it in the microwave but the money caught fire. He called me screaming, asking what to do, and I couldn't help but laugh at him.

Uncle Jimmy managed to get on the radar of the NFL. After practice one day, I got called into Coach Meyer's office, and some guys from the NFL were there. Classic white men in suits. They told me that Uncle Jimmy was a known gangster, that the FBI had been watching him, that they didn't want me hanging around him.

I nodded yes but then blew them off. Screw them, Uncle Jimmy was family. Having him around made me feel more comfortable. Because it's not like Indianapolis was exactly hospitable to Black people.

◆

About that racism.

Indiana is infamous for it. There was a time in the 1920s when an estimated 30 percent of native-born white men in the state were members of the Ku Klux Klan. Back then, the Klan controlled the state government—right on up to the governor, who was close friends with the Grand Wizard.

Which brings me to Bob Irsay. Even if he hadn't been a racist, nobody would've had any respect for the guy. We'd see the way he'd get liquored up and talk to his son Jimmy, who's now the Colts owner: he'd always snap at him and humiliate him and tell him to shut the fuck up. Jimmy was completely under his dad's thumb when I was there. Everyone knows he has had his own issues with substance abuse, but he's not like his dad. Jimmy was a good-hearted guy. He'd been a linebacker at SMU before I was there, so he knew football too, which is probably why the Colts organization is so well run now.

But back then? With Bob in charge, it was one of those cases in sports where the owner sets the tone for the whole organization. And something was rotten from the head on down.

I still think about Irsay's racist joke at his Christmas party, when he came up to me and some other Black guys and said, *You got a kike, you got a wetback, and you got a nigger. . .*

I said, *Fuck that,* and walked away.

It was so demeaning because I knew exactly what he was thinking: *I'm a rich white man, these niggers work for me; this is my party and I can say whatever I want.* And back then, he could. I didn't say anything about it afterward because I had no recourse. The media either wouldn't have believed me or would've swept it under the rug and chalked it up to a harmless joke.

To me, that incident says a lot about the mindset of sports owners. That mentality is much more common than people think. Donald Sterling, the Clippers owner who got forced out of the league for his racist comments? He was just the unlucky one who got caught.

The Colts had a racist owner, which was fitting because Indianapolis was a fundamentally racist place. Now, I hesitate to paint Indy

with too broad a brush. I met some great people there—my life partner Penny is from there, though I met her later—and my parents always told me that there are good people and bad people of every color
in every place. But let me put it this way: being in Indianapolis made
me conscious of being Black in a way that even growing up in Texas in
the 1960s did not. All the history with the Klan? You *felt* that. There
was an edge to that place, a sense of danger. All the brothers knew the
places we just shouldn't go: anywhere with a *ville* or a *burg* in it, especially Brownsburg (which is why those women were so crazy for us).
It was almost like going through a time warp to the bad old days my
parents used to tell me about.

I had heard about the Klan stuff but had mostly put it out of my
mind my first year or so there. Until 1988, when I turned on the TV
and saw all these guys in white robes and hoods, having a huge rally
right in the downtown area. I was floored: I grew up in the South in the
'60s and you never saw stuff like that.

◆

It turned out that the '87 season was the high-water mark in Indy. We
were 9–6 that year and won the division. But in our playoff game, we
ran into a good Cleveland team, one that should have gone to the Super Bowl if not for Earnest Byner's fumble on the goal line in the AFC
Championship, which was followed by another crazy John Elway drive.
Against the Browns, we hung around and the game was tied at halftime,
but they had a powerful offense and they blew the game open in the
second half.

After '87, we treaded water for the next two years with a nucleus
that just needed a few more pieces but never got them. In '88, we went
9–7 but missed the playoffs, and in '89, we went 8–8.

By '90, things were obviously headed in the wrong direction, but
I faced a dilemma: the Colts were willing to give me the contract I'd
been asking for, north of $10 million for over four years. I was incred-
ibly conflicted. They were offering me top dollar to play the sport I'd

always loved, and still did, to some extent. The problem was I didn't love it *there*—and being there was about to get a lot worse.

I signed the contract during our bye week when we were 2–3. I put on a happy face and tried to convince myself that our team could really do some things. Three weeks later, after our third straight loss moved us to 2–6, I knew I was in a bad situation.

Why did things nose-dive in Indy? It all began with the Jeff George trade. To get Jeff, we gave up Chris Hinton (one of the best offensive linemen in the league) and Andre Rison (one of the top young receivers in the league), along with our first-rounder in the next year's draft.

Don't get me wrong here: I say this as someone who really likes Jeff, both as a person and a quarterback. Jeff always got a bad rap because he was standoffish with the media, but he was the opposite of how they made him out to be. He was cool and funny, the type of white guy who gets along with Black guys. He'd go out clubbing with the brothers, mullet and all.

But he walked into such a bad situation in Indianapolis that he never got the chance to develop the way he deserved. Because the team was depleted by the talent they gave up to get him, Jeff and I got the brunt of the blame as the highest-profile players, whether that was fair or not. The media got on him and he didn't react the way they wanted him to, so he was branded from that point on. I knew the feeling.

Jeff's career is the perfect example of how much in the league depends on circumstances beyond your control. I see Patrick Mahomes with Andy Reid, or Josh Allen and Lamar Jackson with some of the great coaching they've gotten, and I can't help thinking that Jeff— with how accurate he was, with that strong arm that could squeeze the ball in anywhere—would have had an entirely different career if he were in the right situation. As it was, he was surrounded by too few talented players and too many guys there to collect a check.

The scene during those last couple years with the Colts—1990 and 1991—was the most poisonous atmosphere I'd ever been around. We'd lose, and you'd hear guys after the game actually saying that they didn't care because they'd get paid either way. One of those years, after we lost a couple straight games, I called a team meeting and basically called out a lot of guys, not by name—*Don't y'all have pride?*—and I remember realizing at the time how much it was falling on deaf ears. As a running back, the guy taking punishment on every play, I really, really didn't like hearing that shit, because the next week, I'd have to go put my body on the line again. Another day, another dollar for them. For me, any of those days could've been the last of my career.

Before the '91 season, *Sports Illustrated* did a cover story on me headlined "One Happy Camper." I said all the right things in the piece, but I was lying. By that point I knew I'd made a mistake by signing that extension with the Colts.

I realized then how much I'd taken the camaraderie with the Rams for granted. The Rams were a *team*. The Colts were a collection of guys, many of whom didn't want to be there. Guys knew exactly how much everyone was making—I've never seen so much *jealousy*. At the time, we didn't have an established quarterback who could be a leader—a constant in my career—so there was a vacuum of leadership filled by some bad guys.

Like Ray Donaldson, our center. He was a talented player but was lazy and bitter, and his attitude carried over to other offensive linemen. Those last two years, some of the apathy guys on that line showed was just disgraceful. I'd once said that running behind that O-line was like playing Russian roulette, or fighting in Vietnam with a BB gun, and I got a hard time in the media for it. But when you see that apathy, and it's *your* safety that's being compromised, you feel compelled to say something.

Kevin Call was another O-lineman who had some talent but was soft, and not a guy you wanted to go to battle with. We were playing the Giants in 1990 in a Monday night game, the year they won their second Super Bowl, with that ferocious defense with L. T., Carl Banks, and Leonard Marshall. I was trash-talking with one of the guys on the Giants when Kevin pulled me aside and screamed at me: *Eric, stop arguing—you're gonna piss 'em off!* What a coward. I couldn't believe my fucking ears.

In 1990 we went 7–9, the first time a team of mine had finished with a losing record. The next year, the bottom fell out and we went 1–15.

The moment that typified that '91 season came against the Bills, when we were getting blown out and I was getting pounded into the turf play after play. After one play, Bruce Smith helped me up. He had a look of compassion and concern in his eyes I'd never seen on an opponent's face before.

—*Dick, man, you better get down. Those guys aren't blocking us— you're gonna get hurt out here.*

During that game, in the huddle, when he realized how much I was getting killed, Jeff said, *Fuck this, we gotta throw the ball.* Like I said, people don't see these things, but Jeff was a really good guy.

Jeff saw something that fans don't see: that being a running back is like being sent out into a pack of rabid dogs, whose mentality is, *How dare you try to run up in here!* The violence a running back endures is something that fans can't possibly appreciate from the comforts of the stands or the couch. There's really no way to describe the speed, viciousness, and danger of the sport at a professional level. Playing running back in the NFL is like running full-speed, with your eyes closed, into a brick wall about thirty times—and having other walls, from other directions, slam into you as well.

It's like getting into a car crash on every carry. Like a car crash, each carry has the potential to leave you permanently disfigured. Like a car crash, sometimes you don't realize the damage until a few hours, or even a few days, later. Like a car crash, some hits stay with you for decades: when I was with the Colts, I scored a touchdown against the Jets in New York, but after I crossed the plane I let my guard down and a linebacker popped me in the chest, and our teams got into a fight. I don't even remember the guy's name, but it wasn't until about fifteen years ago that my chest stopped hurting in that exact spot I was hit.

People who think they know what it's like will say, *But I played in high school!* Guess what? I did too, and there's no comparison. High school games were fun! I used to look forward to them all week. In the pros, it takes every second of the week to prepare your body and your mind for the next game.

As I got older, after I left the Rams, it became harder and harder to prepare my mind. I'd take my Darvocet painkiller, which calmed my nerves a little bit, but on some days, you just can't get your mind to where it needs to be. Some days, being human wins out. Regardless of how much money they're paying you, regardless of how good you are, you're gonna have days when carrying the ball thirty times is the last thing in the world you wanna do. That's one of many dirty little secrets of the NFL: on any given Sunday, a huge percentage of guys out there would rather be doing anything else.

For me, the task grew harder after a game in 1988, when Bears defensive lineman Dan Hampton kicked me in the head by accident and messed up my neck. I'd always had a premonition I'd break my neck playing football. After that injury, I *felt* that premonition viscerally.

But still I always played hard. Even when I hated being out there, I played hard. Even while my longtime fear of breaking my neck surfaced with more and more frequency, I played hard. You really don't have a choice: there's just too much on the line on every play, and those guys on the other side are playing hard.

Plus, it's not just *your* safety at stake. It's also that of your teammates, and you have to show up, for them, on every single play. I don't want to get into the football-military comparisons, because playing a football game isn't remotely the same as fighting in a war, but I once met a military guy who was volunteering to go back for his *fourth* tour of duty overseas. I was blown away by his courage, and I asked him why he was volunteering to do that, and he threw it back at me: *If your teammates are out there, don't you* have *to be out there with them*, he asked me? The answer is yes.

When I heard that John Shaw had said that football players are like horses, and that they'll run when you open the gate even if they're unhappy, it pissed me off for a million reasons, and still does. But that doesn't mean he wasn't right.

•

Once things with the Colts began to fall apart, a lot of the blame came my way as the team's marquee player. It was real vitriol, stuff that still hurts. A lot of it was clearly motivated by racism.

One time, Fredd Young and I were walking down the street and a white woman approached us.

—*Are you Eric Dickerson?*

—*Yeah.*

—*You're not worth the money they're paying you.*

I went crazy, cursing her out, calling her a fucking bitch. Nowadays I'd probably call her a "Karen."

Then there was that game in 1990 when the fans hung a racist banner. It featured a Black baby in my number 29 jersey, wearing red lipstick, holding a fried chicken leg, with a stack of money on one side and a watermelon on the other.

I saw it before the game during warmups and it felt like someone socked me in the stomach. Some of the other Black guys were laughing. Like I said, that team had a lot of jealous people, and jealous people like it when someone more successful than them is made to feel bad. I remember thinking at the time: *Laugh now, but you're next. That's what they think of* all *of us.*

I pointed it out to my buddy, Jeff Herrod, who was horrified: *Man, what the hell is that?*

I said, *Let's see how long it takes for them to take it down.*

It stayed up until almost halftime.

After that, in another game, the Indianapolis fans hung dolls with my jersey in effigy from the stands. I thought, *What's next, a lynching?*

In 1989, the Hoosier Dome crowd booed me when I surpassed 10,000 yards for my career, breaking Jim Brown's record for how quickly I did it. I did it in 91 games—the next fastest was Brown, with 98—and I'm incredibly proud of that record because it shows that in my prime, nobody has ever been better than me. At the same time, I'm still pissed off that the Colts fans tarnished that moment for me. It's inconceivable that they would have booed a white player who'd broken an important, long-standing NFL record.

Years later, when I gave my Hall of Fame speech, I said that despite everything, I was proud to wear the horseshoe on my helmet, and that's true. The older I get, the more I appreciate the history of the sport. The Colts have a proud history, and though it's mostly from before and after the time I was there, we did win a division title, and I'd like to think I was a part of that tradition.

But that town has a lot of bad memories for me. The Irsay slur, that banner, the boos, the Klan rally: these things don't fade away with time.

I'm sixty-one years old now. Do I see myself ever setting foot in Indianapolis again, for as long as I live? No.

◆

One of the other casualties of the bad situation in Indianapolis was Ron Meyer, who was fired in 1991 in the middle of the season.

Ron was such a great coach at SMU because he was great at two things: motivating players and recruiting them. Both were a testament to his personality, but as a pure X's and O's guy, he was average. In Indy, the players weren't capable of being motivated, and that was it for Ron, who was fired after we lost our first five games to start the year.

I was sad for him and thought he deserved better. Through all the bullshit, he was one guy in the organization that I trusted and liked, the one guy who made showing up for work tolerable. Ron had always been a people pleaser—that's what made him such a great recruiter, ever since he showed up to my house in Sealy—but in Indy, he was in an unwinnable situation: he wanted to win games, he wanted the players to be happy, he wanted Bob Irsay to be happy. As a college coach, it's your show, so you have control, but in the pros so many things were out of his control, and by the end, he seemed defeated and beaten down.

They replaced Ron with Rick Venturi, the defensive coordinator, who was completely unqualified and only got the job because he was a classic company man who'd been kissing the Irsays' asses for years and, a lot of us thought, trying to undermine Ron. I talked to Ron afterward and he didn't want to get into the politics of everything. He just said, *Eric, be careful.*

The writing was on the wall for me. My rushing totals had gone from 1,659 in '88 to 1,311 in '89, to 677 in '90, and then 536 in '91. Things were going south between me and the fans, and between me and the organization. Before the 1990 season, I held out, and Jim Irsay suspended me a few games.

In '91, things blew up in practice when we were 0–9 and my hamstring—which bothered me throughout my career—started barking at me in practice. I told a trainer, who told me to go in for treatment, so I left the field. But Venturi had a tantrum about it and made it out like I'd just left because I didn't want to be there. Then, they wanted me to get a physical, but by that point I didn't trust the organization at all, so I got an independent doctor, who told me what I knew: I had a strained hamstring.

But Venturi suspended me anyway for "conduct detrimental to the team," which was bullshit. I think he knew the only chance to keep his head coaching job was if he did some drastic shit, and he used me for that. Like I said, Indianapolis in those years was just a toxic work environment. You *felt* those office politics. Ron was right to tell me to watch out.

This is how bad things got with the Colts that year: during my suspension, I got really, really sick, and was running an extremely high fever on game day. I could barely stand up, but the Colts insisted I come to the dome for the game. I came in and they took my temperature, I guess because they didn't believe me. Only when it came up 104 did they let me go home.

After all that, there was no chance I was going back. After the season, they kicked Venturi back to his defensive coordinator role and hired a new head coach, Ted Marchibroda, who'd been the offensive coordinator of the explosive Bills. Marchibroda called me on the phone and said he wanted me back, that we could turn this thing around, but by that point I'd made up my mind. I was scheduled to make $3 million, but I took a $1.5 million pay cut just to get out of there.

CHAPTER 13

IT'S AL DAVIS'S WORLD—AND I'M JUST LIVING IN IT

I went back the next season to L.A. My adopted home. The city where football had last been *fun*, before all the bullshit took over.

After it became obvious I was leaving Indianapolis, the Rams tried to get me, hoping for a happy reunion. But there was too much bad blood there. I wasn't trying to go back to Anaheim Stadium, where the fans had thrown fake money at me. I wasn't trying to play for John Shaw, who'd screwed me over at every turn.

But the Raiders seemed like a good fit. They've always had the reputation for being the NFL's island of lost souls, rescuing veterans from bad situations and bringing out the best in them. Before they brought me in, they told me they planned to trade Marcus Allen and that I'd have a clear path to the starting running back job. Back in L.A. as the starter for a storied organization? Sounded good to me.

But it didn't work out that away. That place was a circus from the beginning. Team owner Al Davis's fingerprints were on absolutely everything.

Soon after coming to camp, I learned they had no intention of trading Marcus. In fact, I think Al brought me in just to fuck with Marcus because he hated him so much. That season, I started most of the games but only got 187 carries, which was way short of the featured back role I'd been promised. I wasn't able to get into a rhythm, rushing for only 729 yards while averaging 3.9 yards per carry. The team was disappointing too: after making the playoffs for two straight years, we went 7–9.

The problem was Al. You just couldn't get away from him. A weird play call would come in, and guys would start speculating: Was Al calling plays down from the owner's box again? Things would change on a dime according to his whims, which made everyone feel unsettled all the time. One game, I had nearly 100 yards at half-time—and then sat the bench the entire second half, because Al said so. He'd been a football innovator in the past, but by '92, he had already started to lose it, and we all knew the organization was being held hostage by someone who wasn't totally in his right mind. That remained the case long after I left.

His feud with Marcus was a good example. Like a lot of people, I never knew what Al's problem with Marcus was. Like a lot of people, I'd heard the rumors: that Marcus sometimes dated white women, which bothered Al. I'd also heard that Al had never wanted to draft Marcus—why he did, I have no idea—and the two of them had never gotten along.

Whatever the reason, his feud with Marcus was batshit crazy. Around the facility, he wouldn't speak to him or even acknowledge him. Years later, when Marcus made the Hall of Fame, the two of them ran into each other and Marcus decided to bury the hatchet, or at the very least keep up polite appearances, and he reached out to shake Al's hand. Al snubbed him. All he said was, *I can't do that.* I have no idea what he meant by that, but that pisses me off: without guys like Marcus Allen, Al Davis doesn't get into the Hall of Fame. But that's pro sports for you: owners call all the shots, and even when they go crazy and run a franchise into the ground for decades, they can be Hall of Famers.

With Al at the top, we were a dysfunctional team, and on dysfunctional teams, you'll find teammates pitted against each other. That was definitely the case with Marcus and me. He's now my close friend and my golfing buddy, but we got off on the wrong foot as teammates. Before the season, Roger Craig, who I'd been friends with since the Hula

Bowl in college, told me, *Watch out for Marcus—he'll backstab you.*
That year, I came to learn Marcus was talking shit behind my back,
and I hated him for it. It took me a long time, but I forgave him and
realized he acted like he did because of the environment he was in.

It was a bad year, and it ended in the worst way possible. We were
playing at Washington, and before the game, out of nowhere, the
coaches told me that Marcus and I were going to dress but not play
because they wanted to take a long look at Nick Bell, a young running back they'd drafted the year before. That game, Marcus got just 5
carries and I rode the bench the entire time. It showed how the Raiders had gone from an organization that revived careers to the football
equivalent of an elephant graveyard. Picture that scene: Eric Dickerson and Marcus Allen, two Hall of Fame running backs, sitting on the
bench the whole game.

Our bench was right in front of the stands at RFK Stadium, and
I'll never forget the humiliation of sitting there. I was a great athlete,
a proud athlete, but there I was, a benchwarmer. I remembered being
in seventh grade and running for those touchdowns in my first game.
I remembered those days at SMU, when I felt like a man among boys.
I remembered my first few years in the pros and how the air felt on
my face as I ran for touchdowns. It hadn't been that long ago when I
loved the sport and everything about it. But sitting on that bench that
day, watching my team win a game I couldn't have cared less about, I
realized I now despised it.

◆

That year with the Raiders I suffered a neck injury that ultimately
ended my career. Coming into that season, when I turned thirty-two,
I thought I had three, maybe four years left: I didn't have my acceleration from a few years before but I still had my feet, my feel for the
game, and my power. But the neck injury did me in. 1993 would be my
last season, and it wasn't much of a season: I played in four games and
had just 26 carries.

About the injury: ever since high school, I'd had a premonition of getting paralyzed on the field. It was so bad I had recurring nightmares about it. I also mentioned the time in 1988, when Dan Hampton of the Bears accidentally kicked me in the head, which caused it to snap back and wrench my neck. After that, the premonition seemed more real and I felt more vulnerable than ever. It got harder and to shove my fears to the back of my mind, and all the while, my love for the sport was fading fast.

Fast-forward to '92, my Raiders season: We were playing the Chiefs and I was carrying the ball around the edge when a defensive back dove at my ankle to tackle me. I tried to leap over him but didn't quite clear him, so I flipped in the air and landed on my head. I felt a burning sensation under my left shoulder blade up through my neck. It was very painful, but the Raiders doctors said it was just a "burner," which is common enough in football. I played through it and didn't think much of it.

But it didn't go away for days, and then for weeks. Later, I'd learn it was a protruding disc; in other words, my neck was seriously fucked up. It was recklessly unsafe to play any contact sport, let alone play as a running back in the NFL.

But the Raiders' team doctors insisted it was just a burner. They said it was a minor, everyday thing that would go away. I can't prove this, but in retrospect I think they knew the injury was a lot worse than it was but intentionally downplayed it. That's the way that organization was. That's the way the NFL was, and still is.

The injury coincided with when I stopped getting regular playing time, and because I wasn't playing, I didn't quite realize how bad my neck was. I knew it didn't feel normal in practice, but a thirty-two-year-old running back never feels 100 percent. I trusted the doctors and played through it and finished up the season.

That offseason, my neck still didn't feel right. What stung worse, however, was the memory of that last game at Washington. I couldn't accept that riding the bench at RFK Stadium was how my career would end, so I signed with the Atlanta Falcons because I'd have a chance to start for them.

It was a big mistake. I can honestly say I'm lucky I got through that year with the ability to walk.

The Falcons' coach, Jerry Glanville, was an idiot, a clown who had no business being an NFL coach. He was known for his stupid, attention-seeking stunts: he'd leave tickets for Elvis Presley at the box office and dress in all-black outfits and a black cowboy hat. He was one of those football guys trying way too hard to be a tough guy, even though he'd never played the game past the small college level and players saw right through his shit. Still, he never stopped trying to prove himself, so he had his players take cheap shots at opponents. I suspected as much when his Oilers players were hitting me after the whistle in my record-breaking game in 1984, and I confirmed it when I played under him. He also ran punishing practices, making his players hit the shit out of each other in training camp, and it was during one of these practices that my neck injury got aggravated.

I was the starting running back the first couple games that season, but I didn't feel right at all. Something terrifying was happening: at random times, my legs would start feeling wobbly; the feeling would come and go. On one play early that season, I got tackled normally, but when I got up, my legs went 90 percent numb, and I felt completely wobbly, like I was walking on a merry-go-round. Carrying the ball in an NFL game is scary enough when you have the full use of your legs. That year, I felt like I had a disability, but I was playing the most violent sport at the highest possible level. It was seriously dangerous.

But I didn't say anything. By that point I knew my career was hanging by a thread and I didn't want it to end. Football was all I'd known. The unknown of not being a football player anymore was even scarier than playing on wobbly legs.

A few games into that season, once it became clear that the Falcons were in for a losing season and committed to younger players, they traded me to the Packers. My running backs coach with the Rams, Gil Haskell, was now with the Packers, and he told me they were excited about teaming me with Mike Holmgren and Brett Favre, who were in their second year together and obviously heading for great things. I was happy to get out of Atlanta and still thought I could contribute. But during the physical, the Packers took an MRI of my neck and didn't like what they saw.

They sent me to a specialist in Green Bay, who didn't mince words. He told me my next hit could be my last, and that I should never play football again.

—*You'll either die on the field, or you'll be paralyzed from the neck down*, he said. *It's not a matter of if. It's a matter of when.*

In retrospect, given how I felt, I shouldn't have been shocked, but of course I was. Up until that moment, I was under the impression I'd play for three more years or so, and maybe get in a couple of 1,300-yard seasons: not me at my peak, but still a damn good player. Then the doctor delivered the news, telling me I was lucky I wasn't in a wheelchair.

Still, I clung to hope. I clung to my identity as a football player. Injury had been a foreign concept to me during my career: I had the toe issue in '84, and I had some problems with my hamstrings, but other than that I'd been blessed with great health. The idea that I was physically unable to keep going was hard to wrap my head around. I flew out to L.A. to see Dr. Robert Watkins, a renowned sports spine specialist, hoping he'd clear me. But he didn't. In the strongest possible terms, he told me that I should retire.

I didn't push back. It was over.

They say that athletes die twice: once when they retire, and then again when they actually die. I felt that. The athlete in me was gone forever, and I mourned that loss. It's like the grieving process for any death: there's shock, and sadness, and the feeling that it's just not fair.

But there was also tremendous relief. I'd been trying so hard to hang on that I didn't realize that the thrill I'd once felt playing the game was long gone. It had been pushed aside in my heart by bitterness and contempt. Toward the John Shaws. The Al Davises. The doctors with the Raiders. The Jerry Glanvilles. The writers. And yes, even some of the fans, like the ones who hung that racist banner, or threw money at me, or sent me that hate mail.

When I showed up to Rams practice in 1983 as a wide-eyed rookie, thrilled to be there and loving every minute of it, the veterans would tell me football was an ugly business. *Just wait*, they said. I didn't believe them at the time, but after eleven years in the league, I did.

CHAPTER 14

THE GOLD JACKET—AND THE RESPONSIBILITY THAT COMES WITH IT

I wish I could say that after I retired, I felt nothing but relief. That I walked away freely and happily into the next phase of life. But no. Retirement was tough. All of a sudden I had so much time and no idea how to fill it. Football had given me structure and meaning for as long as I could remember. Now it was gone, and for the first time in my life, I felt lost.

Ever since I'd started playing, whenever football season would come along in late summer, I'd *smell* it in the air. I'd smell the grass, the sweat, the equipment, the adrenaline. The smell would activate my body, telling me it was time to get into gear. After I retired, I smelled that smell for many, many years, and I felt my body get ready for the game. But there was no game. It was like being an amputee and feeling a phantom limb.

Yes, I hated the sport by the end, but I couldn't help thinking the end came too quickly. I felt like a failure, like I hadn't accomplished everything I should have. Because I'd planned to play another couple of years, being forced to retire, not on my terms, felt like a failure to accomplish a goal. It's a mentality all great athletes have: we're always striving for *more,* and because of that, we're always falling short of the mark. It took me years to get to the point where I could look back on my career with pride. I know that seems strange, but I had to wait until the disappointment in myself faded in order to appreciate my accomplishments.

Even though the game brought back negative emotions, I still couldn't pull myself away from it those first few years. I'd watch games, and running backs in particular, and wonder why they were out there and I wasn't. I remember watching Emmitt Smith racking up stats behind that great Dallas line and being jealous. *Shit,* I'd think to myself. *I can do what he's doing.*

But it was obvious my body wasn't right at all. Dr. Watkins had told me that despite the condition of my neck, I didn't need surgery, and that physical therapy should take me back to normal in terms of day-to-day functioning. But it took a long time to get there. For about a year after I retired, it was literally too painful to lie down, so I slept horribly. Whatever sleep I got, I got while sitting up in a chair. I wasn't in a good place emotionally during that time, and I'm sure being constantly sleep-deprived contributed to that.

Finances made me anxious as well: I went from making seven figures to making zero. All the while, I still had my house to pay off, and I was still fighting with my daughter's mother in court over money. (I'll get into that situation a bit more later.) I was a retiree but I was also a guy in my mid-thirties, and being cut off from your income, just like that, is a shock. I'm just grateful I had the parents I had, who drilled into me the importance of being smart about my money. I was the exception to the rule on that one: I've seen a lot of guys live paycheck to paycheck their whole careers and go into debt almost immediately afterward. There but for the grace of God—and the wisdom of Viola and Kary—go I.

I knew being idle would make me depressed, so I tried to keep myself busy, but nothing I did was anywhere near as satisfying as playing football. When you're that good at something that once brought you so much joy, it's deflating when other things don't give you the same payoff.

First, I was a partner in a modeling and talent agency called Paragon Talent. It did well for a little while, but then one of the partners got greedy and did some shady shit that basically torpedoed the agency, so that was that. There are snakes in the business world just like there are in the NFL.

After that, in 2000, I got hired by Monday Night Football as a sideline reporter—and was terrible at it. I love football and I love talking about it, but it just wasn't the job for me. I wasn't good at getting those little human-interest details, and I had no qualifications or talent for the job. I lasted two seasons, and after it was over, my confidence in my ability to present myself on TV was badly shaken, and I spent more than a decade mostly out of the public eye.

◆

In the years since I retired, I've watched the highlights of my career dozens of times: you can't avoid them. Sometimes, I'll transport myself in my mind to the feeling of breaking a long run, and the familiar sensations come back: the crowd is just background noise, but mostly I'm hearing the sound of my breathing and of my pads clacking gently. Knowing you can outrun everybody—that's the best feeling in the world.

But most of the time, when I see those highlights, I feel like I'm watching a different guy out there. Drayton once asked me bluntly: *What's it like to have once been such a great athlete, and now be an old man?* I answered that it feels surreal that it all happened so fast. It's one of those things that bowls you over and gets you thinking about life and loss and mortality, like when you're in the mall and you think, out of nowhere, *In a hundred years, all of these people are gonna be dead.* That guy in the highlights, running fluidly and making it look as easy as opening the door? The guy who'll you'll never, ever see looking back once he gets in the open field because he knows nobody can catch him? He's gone, forever.

In his place is this old man. I didn't put on a hundred pounds like a lot of guys, and I have to say I look pretty good, outwardly. But if you look under the hood you'll see the game took a toll—on my body, on my mind—like it does on all of us. I didn't get out unscathed.

My brain. I've discussed it with other ex-players: we'll have thoughts that are just not normal thoughts for a person to have. My temper can be really, really short, and it scares me. Someone will say something, a little thing, and I'll think, *I just wanna hit him in his fucking mouth*. And then I go so far as to picture myself doing it before sanity returns and I'm shocked at my own thoughts.

I just pray it doesn't get worse; I pray I don't become the guy who doesn't recognize his kids. That's my greatest fear and it's a real one, based on what I've seen with other guys who have devoted themselves to this game.

I've talked a lot to Tony Dorsett and I talked to Gale Sayers, before he died—all-time great running backs who got hit with these problems later in life. I was talking to Gale a few years ago and he just kept on asking me the same thing, over and over and over. It was incredibly sad. In my mind, Gale was still the beautiful runner from the highlight tapes.

Like every player from my era, and probably today's players too, I've had too many concussions to count, because back then, the only ones we counted were the really bad ones. If it wasn't really bad, you'd call it a ding and you'd get back out on the field. My worst one was in college, my freshman year, when a cornerback from TCU came off the edge and popped me in my earhole. I remember coming to the sideline and saying, *Man, I got hit hard*. The next thing I knew I was in the locker room: I was told later I'd walked off the field in the middle of the next *play*. When we watched it on film later, we all laughed. Now we know it wasn't funny.

But the concussions are just one thing, and focusing on diagnosed concussions mostly misses the point. The fact is, with the violence of the NFL game, your brain is getting knocked around your skull practically on every play, even if it's not an official concussion. This isn't high school football. In the NFL, guys smash heads on every single play—huge guys who are blazingly fast and know how to channel every ounce of force in their bodies.

That's why the NFL has a real problem. All of the so-called safety measures they've put in place really only address the really bad concussions, the ones everyone can see on TV. But that's just window dressing, a way to say they're doing something after their phony doctors denied there was a problem for so many years. The way the league treats its retirees is absolutely shameful, and goes against the "football is family" crap that they peddle. I see the way the league treats the many, many guys who need help. I've seen guys who can't tell you what day it is being forced to fill out a mound of paperwork.

I worry about my cousin, Ricky Seals-Jones, who's becoming a star tight end and definitely has the talent to have a long career. I talk to him and tell him to be careful, but he doesn't want to hear it. *But Eric, I love it!*

I loved it too. But I'm paying the price now. I remember a little after my career ended, I was sitting on a flight from L.A. next to O. J. Simpson. He asked me how my body felt, and I told him that all things considered, I felt fine. He asked me how old I was, and I told him thirty-three. Then he said: *When you turn fifty, those hits are gonna come back to you.*

He was right.

I have a terrible back and I can't sleep on my left side. Sleeping is a real problem for me, as it is for countless ex-football players. It seems like every guy I talk to says the same thing: we wake up throughout the night and almost never get a good night's sleep. Usually I can get through because I'm accustomed to functioning this way, but sometimes it gets really bad. One time I was playing golf after sleeping particularly badly for about a week, and after we finished the round, I was so exhausted my friend had to help me to my car. The moment I got in, I fell asleep.

My toe is in awful shape too, from the turf toe injury in '84. It's crazy to me that I broke the rushing record, and then played nearly a decade more in the NFL, with an injury that causes me so much pain to this day. I wrote before about the time I dropped a golf ball on it and couldn't move for a few minutes after that. Most guys who played in the league have something like that, disabilities big and small that the rest of the world doesn't see.

My mom always told me that football was too violent, that she didn't want me playing it. When I got to the pros, she'd constantly say, *They don't care about you,* where the *you* meant my long-term health. I had no idea how much football would catch up to me later. As with most things, my mom was right.

I think about my ten-year-old son, too, who I swear is a better natural athlete than me and will excel in any sport he plays. He plays flag football now and he's outstanding. If he wants to play tackle football when he's older, I won't love it but I won't stop him. If he loves the sport like I did, I don't feel I have the right to make that decision for him. But I'm praying he chooses another sport.

So the big question: Would I play again, given everything I know now?

Yes—if I was in the same predicament of trying to help my mother financially. My mom had worked since she was a little girl because that's what you did back in those days. She and my dad brought me up and turned me into something, unlike a lot of the guys I grew up with. Even though she didn't want me playing the sport, I loved her so much that providing for her was the most important thing for me, and I'm glad I was able to do it.

But what if money wasn't a factor, and I knew what I knew now about all the injuries, including brain injuries: Would I still play?

Hell no.

◆

Ultimately, I have mixed feelings about the game. All of us do, even the guys who won't admit it, and there are many of them. Football was my life, for better or worse. It did its damage but it also gave me so many positive memories.

Aside from the births of my kids, the proudest accomplishment of my life was being inducted into the Pro Football Hall of Fame in 1999.

I've always been very confident in my abilities, but it still blew my mind to stand up there with the rest of those guys in the gold jackets. It was an honor and also a bonding experience: there are only a handful of people on this planet who know what it's like to walk in the shoes of an NFL Hall of Famer. Only we know how hard we've worked, the obstacles we've overcome, the inner drive it took to get us to this point, how blessed we are with our talent but also the challenges that come with it. Being around those guys felt like being welcomed into a community that stretches back through time. There was something spiritual about putting on that gold jacket.

Before my speech, Jackie Slater introduced me at the podium. I chose Jackie because I wanted to share the accomplishment with my Rams offensive linemen. My success had always been their success, and Jackie—who'd get inducted into the Hall of Fame himself two years later—represented those guys.

Jackie said that when he first met me in 1983, I was a *focused young man, a rookie with something to prove.* I appreciated that a lot, because that's what I was: I might have made it look easy, but I was driven to excel.

He also described me as someone with *an unshaken loyalty to his family and friends.* I'm glad he said that: loyalty is the quality of mine I'm most proud of. The person who the media often presented isn't close to the same person my friends and family know. The real me is the guy Jackie described.

In my speech I thanked Jackie and a lot of those Rams linemen by name. I thanked Drayton. I thanked Ron Meyer and George Owen.

I also thanked my friend Hollie Frey, who I consider my best friend along with Drayton. We dated for a while during my career and then went on to become great friends. I wasn't the best boyfriend to Hollie—one woman wasn't enough for me back then—but our relationship has worked perfectly since we became friends. Hollie was the one who first sounded the alarm about my neck injury. There's a good chance that without her, I would've been in denial about how serious it was and pushed through it, so I owe her my health, if not my life. She has been by my side through everything, including that racist banner they hung in the Hoosier Dome, which hurt her as much as it hurt me. She's an incredibly caring person; I couldn't imagine my life without her.

And, of course, I thanked my family. My mom was ninety-four at the time and couldn't travel to Canton, Ohio, but I was glad she was alive to appreciate my accomplishment. She made me a tough-minded, proud person who would never settle for anything less than my best. It was ironic that she hated football but gave me the qualities it took to be great at it. My dad had been dead for more than twenty years at the time of my induction, and he never saw me play college or pro ball. But in my speech, I recounted a time in high school when he came to watch me practice and sat in the stands reading his Bible. After practice, he pulled me aside and said, *Son, let me tell you something. This is great, but I want you to understand one thing: You can gain the world, but don't lose your soul.*

He knew I was good, and that football would take me places, but he wanted to make sure I stayed true to the person he and my mom were raising me to be. Standing on that podium in my gold jacket, I believed *that* was my proudest accomplishment.

◆

But being a Hall of Famer doesn't mean you ride off into the sunset and live happily ever after. Guys are struggling—many of us badly, *all* of us more than we let on. To build this league into what it is, we sacrificed our bodies. For many of us, despite the fact that we were led to believe otherwise, we sacrificed our minds.

Yet the health benefits for retired players are pathetic: under the most recent Collective Bargaining Agreement, guys who've played three years in the league get health benefits for five years after they retire. After that, they're cut off. That's a problem, because the damage from the game takes years and sometimes decades to show up. When guys really need those benefits, they're long gone.

Compare that to retired Major League Baseball players: a baseball player who has been on a big-league roster for one day gets health insurance for the rest of his life.

Does race have something to do with it? You better believe it. The NFL's business model is to wring out as much profit as possible from us, and then discard our Black bodies and dust off their hands. We're out of sight, out of mind.

It's not right, and I'm trying to do something about it. For the past couple of years, I've been working with other Hall of Famers to advocate for lifetime health benefits for *all* retired NFL players. We're the guys who made the league what it was, but the league treats us like yesterday's trash.

The NFL would say it's too expensive to insure us. They'd say we knew about the dangers of the sport when we signed up. But that's bullshit. For decades, the league hid the dangers from us and the public, spending God knows how much money on junk science and PR campaigns.

Too expensive? Please. This is a league with a commissioner making $40 million a year. This is the league that's currently developing a Hall of Fame Village in Canton expected to cost $1 billion. This NFL prints money—and that's because of the *players*, both past and present.

I talk to a lot of ex-teammates and fellow Hall of Famers, and about 85 to 90 percent of them suffer from some kind of cognitive decline. Mostly, they suffer in silence. A few years ago, an ex-teammate called me and asked, *Hey man, how you doing?*

I said I was good.

Then he said, *No, really, how you doing? Because I'm not good.*

I said I was okay, but not great, and we got talking about the stuff most guys keep to themselves: Forgetting things. Spells of depression, out of nowhere. Uncontrollable rages about the littlest things. He told me that in the middle of the day, at random times, he'll break down crying for no reason.

The NFL keeps this stuff out of the public eye. They're helped by the retired players themselves, who are too proud to have people see them in their current states. As football players, we're taught not to show weakness. We'd rather people know us from our highlights, not as the broken old men we've become.

So we stay quiet, letting the league continue to make money off us. They show our highlights, they sell our jerseys, they trot us out at halftime to smile and wave and pretend everything's okay. The NFL's marketing slogan is "Football is family," and guys go along with it.

But not me. I think it's time to stand up. It might not be a popular position—a lot of fans will say we knew what we were getting into, that we made big salaries *playing a kid's game*—but it's the right thing to do. People are suffering and we need to do something about it.

In my opinion, the league has driven a wedge between current players and retired players. Gene Upshaw, executive director of the NFL Players Association until his death in 2008, went along with that, and now his successor, DeMaurice Smith, is doing that too. The NFLPA's leaders have always seen their responsibility as being to the active players, and they don't want to split the pie with the retired guys, so they cut the retired guys out.

But here's the thing: the current players are screwing themselves over, even if they don't realize it. They're young and they feel invincible, and they think they're gonna play forever. But on average, they'll play just 3.3 years. When DeMaurice Smith tells them they don't owe anything to these old guys, they have to realize they're gonna be those old guys a lot sooner than they think.

But that's the NFL: the league has successfully divided and conquered the current and retired players. The consequences are the thousands of tragedies most people don't see: the guys who don't recognize their kids. The wives who are left to pick up the pieces of their husbands' shattered lives.

During his speech at my Hall of Fame induction, Jackie talked about my loyalty to my family and friends. To me, the brotherhood of retired NFL players is my family. Fighting for them is my responsibility.

CHAPTER 15

GOD AND DEATH

Something else made retirement hard: my mom died in 2000.
She was ninety-five years old. Her mind was as sharp as ever but her body had betrayed her. She said that if she had another body, she could go on. But with the body she was in, she was tired.

—*All my friends are gone,* she told me. *God must have forgotten about me. I'm just stuck here.*

She was ready. I was not. At her funeral, I collapsed to my knees at her casket and wept uncontrollably. The last time I'd cried so hard was at my dad's funeral twenty-two years before. I was seventeen then and I wondered how I could possibly go on. Now I was almost forty and I felt like a lost little boy again. An orphan. It was like I was a boat, and each of my parents was one sail. I'd lost both of my sails and now I was adrift on an ocean. I didn't know which direction to go in or how to even move forward.

I didn't think her death would hit me as hard as it did. I'd gone over it in my mind for decades, because she'd always been older than the parents of my peers. But when it happened, the grief completely overwhelmed me.

I was talking to Drayton about that a few years ago. At the time, his dad was sick and near death. Drayton had been doing lots of thinking about it and he also thought he was ready, but I told him there's no such thing as being ready. I used an example from the Bible: when Lazarus died, Jesus wept, even though he knew he could raise him up. When Drayton's dad finally died, he understood what I meant.

My faith has deepened in the decades since my career. I owe it to my dad, who was the most spiritual, faithful man I've ever been around. The things he'd always tell me, I understood once I got older. When I worried about his health, he'd tell me that our bodies are just shells but that our souls are eternal, and that death is just a part of life. He said he knew he was going to heaven, and he told me to be a good person so we could be there together. Flashing back to a hot day in Sealy in the 1960s, I can still hear his voice: *Eric, this earth, this ain't your home. It's just a stopover before your eternal home.*

He was trying to comfort me, but when I was a kid I didn't want to hear it. Now that I'm older, I feel soothed by his words and I tell my own kids what he told me. They say, *Dad, I don't want to hear about it!* I tell them I used to say the same thing, and that when they're my age and I'm long gone, they'll understand.

I'm a Christian and I believe in God, and I believe God has blessed me. I don't push my religious beliefs on anyone, but I carry that gratitude around every day of my life.

I've said before that my ability to run the football was a gift from God, and I mean that humbly. My natural ability wasn't *me*. It was God. I don't think I'm better than anyone else, I just know I was lucky enough to have gotten a very particular gift.

From the time I was in high school, my family had a spiritual mentor, a man named Stanley LeBlanc, a white man from New Iberia, Louisiana. I grew closer to him after I got into the pros. His whole thing was, *We can do nothing without God.* I took that to heart.

On every major decision I made, I consulted with Stanley. He knew nothing about football but his connection to God was powerful. He told me the Rams would trade up to draft me—and he was right. He told me that despite the punishment I took during games, I'd never get carted off the field or need surgery—and he was right. When I was buying my current house in Calabasas, he told me exactly what to bid on it, even though I loved the house and the bid was low. I bid $1.05 million—and I got the house.

He died in 1990, and I was devastated. But his lessons stayed with me. He would tell me his communication with God was his gift, just like running the football was mine. He had a little catchphrase every time he told me something that was in store for me: *Watch my smoke.*

When it turned out he'd been right, I'd go back to him, and he'd say, *Watch my smoke, boy. I told you I was good.*

He told me that one day, I'd write a book about my career and my life. I was skeptical. He just told me, *Watch my smoke.* This book you're reading is an homage to him.

Stanley LeBlanc is a big part of my faith. So are my life experiences: God has looked out for me in many ways. In college, I got into a car accident, and I spun out and saw an eighteen-wheel truck barreling toward me. It was so close I could see the dirt and dead bugs on its grill, and right then, I was sure that grill was gonna be the last thing I'd ever see. But no. The truck swerved out of the way, and I'm still here today.

In 2018, fires destroyed countless houses in Southern California and in Calabasas. But miraculously, mine was spared.

Another time, I was working on my car and the battery exploded, and the corrosive acid shot out everywhere—except for my eyes. I can still see, and I owe that to God. I have countless stories like these.

My grandfather would always tell me, *God will always bless you because you're good-hearted, and you do things with your heart.* I've tried to be a good person, the person my parents raised me to be. I'd like to think my grandfather was right.

◆

One thing I did with my whole heart was give to my siblings. I have two half-brothers and two half-sisters—all of them Helen's kids, not Viola's—and ever since I signed my first pro contract, I have provided for them. But I came to learn that money can be both a blessing and a curse, and it definitely poisoned my relationship with my siblings.

They were much younger than me and by the time they were teen-agers, I was already an NFL star. Because of that, they always knew me as the guy who *gave them stuff*, and the relationship always had strings attached. For years, I gave and gave, and gave and gave some more. But it was never enough, and they were never able or motivated enough to make anything of themselves. After I retired and had to tighten my belt with money, those relationships got ugly.

Especially with my half-sisters, Tasha and Lisa. They'd grown up in Helen's house, next door from where I lived with Viola and Kary, and things over there were more tumultuous. Helen's husband—his name was Robert but we called him Bobcat—used to beat up Helen when they got into fights.

I remember when I was nine years old, seeing Helen and Bobcat through our window. They were outside their house screaming at each other, and then they started fighting, physically. Helen was wearing a nightgown, and Bobcat just tore it off, leaving her naked, so she ran into our house. Viola told me to go to my room, and then she grabbed her shotgun and walked outside with it, looking for Bobcat. He got away, and eventually he and Helen made up.

But the violence continued. It was really sad, because I liked Bob-cat in a lot of ways. He was an outgoing, fun guy who always treated me well. He didn't fit the profile of an *abuser* and he didn't mistreat Helen in other ways. But he'd seen his own dad beat up his mom when he was a kid, and he grew up thinking it was sort of okay to hit a wom-an. Finally, when I was in the pros, I heard he'd hit Helen again, so I called him up on the phone. I told him this was it: if he wanted to hit someone, he'd have to hit me. He was apologetic, and we talked about how he grew up around that kind of thing. I tried to get it through to him how unacceptable it was, and he at least tried to listen.

Eventually, he and Helen wound up getting divorced. But life is complicated: after that, they stayed really good friends.

Anyway, this was the household my half-siblings grew up in. May-be, because we were so far apart in age and didn't grow up under the same roof, they didn't see me as a brother but rather as a piggy bank.

I gave *everything* to them: school clothes for years, multiple cars, trips to exotic places, even braces when my sister was a teenager. But the more I gave, the more they felt entitled. At a certain point, the way they turned out to be, conflict was inevitable.

It was always something. One time, Tasha had me co-sign the papers for a car she bought—and then stopped making the payments and intentionally didn't tell me, which almost messed up my credit.

Then, after my mom died, they tried to sue me for the house I'd bought her—despite the fact that it was in my name.

Then, Lisa tried to steal a check for $275,000 that I got from one of my investments by intercepting it from the FedEx center. I had to call FedEx myself to make sure she didn't take it. But *that's* the level of some of the stunts they pulled over the years. Just dumb, exhausting shit, one after the next.

They always caused problems with the women I dated. That's common among female relatives of athletes, who assume the women are gold diggers and feel competitive with them. They hated Hollie when we dated, and then they came to hate my life partner Penny. Lisa, who's by far the more unstable of my two sisters, once threatened to put Nair in Penny's shampoo to make her hair fall out.

A lot of the shit they pulled doesn't even sound real, and it feels ridiculous recounting it. Lisa was into witchcraft and all kinds of weird stuff. After we started squabbling over my mom's house after her death, I got a call from a neighbor in Sealy. She told me there was a pentagram on my door, with dead birds, blood, and voodoo dolls on my porch. There was also a sign that said, *No rest, no peace.*

Another time, when tensions were really bad between us, they sent me the meanest, most insane letter imaginable. It said that I'd never done anything for them. That I was only alive because my mama and daddy fucked in the back of a car and had my bastard ass. That even though I'd been successful, they knew the real me, and I was nothing but a bastard.

Mostly, I'd let that stuff roll off my back. It's sad, but at a certain point I realized there was nothing I could do about it. Having crazy-ass people in my family doesn't exactly make me unique.

But what gets me to this day is that my sisters ruined my relationship with Helen. Helen had lupus, and her health was deteriorating rapidly when the stuff with my sisters was escalating. When Lisa tried to steal that $275,000 check, I came to learn that Helen knew about it—and that she was in on it. I was absolutely crushed: my own mom had tried to steal from me.

I called Helen on the phone and screamed at her. I told her that Tasha and Lisa might have been her daughters, but I was her *son*, damn it. I told her, *Don't ever call me again, I'll never call you again*, and then I hung up. That was the last time I ever talked to her. She died about a year later.

I didn't go to her funeral. I was furious with my sisters for a million reasons, and I'd heard they'd been talking about me around town, saying I'd cut Helen off from my money and that Helen died of a broken heart. I knew that if I went to that funeral, things could get really ugly, and I was worried about it. Finally, I had a dream where Viola said to me, *Eric, you don't need to go. And if you do, something bad might happen.* As always, I listened to her and didn't go.

In the years after Helen died, I missed her, and my heart began to soften. I was sad about how things had ended. I came to realize she was weakened, physically and mentally, by the lupus and was blinded by loyalty to her daughters. Tasha and Lisa had pushed her around and scared her, and she didn't know what else to do. My anger began to thaw into pity, and sadness. I missed her.

Then, maybe three or four years after her death, I was going through a drawer and saw a card Helen had sent me for my birthday a few years before she died. I'd never opened it—sometimes I just don't open mail, and then I forget about it—but there it was, so I opened it and read what she wrote. She told me she loved me, and that she just wanted to tell me what a good son I was. She said God had blessed her with me, and not just because I was a football player. She said that one day pretty soon, the angel of death would take her away, but that I could always open this card and know how she felt about me.

I broke down crying. I knew that the feelings in the card were how she really felt about me, and all the stuff that went down in her last years were just things that had escaped her control. She loved me, I loved her, and I forgave her. It's sad her time on Earth ended the way it did, but we'll see each other on the other side.

CHAPTER 16

THE UNLIKELY FAMILY MAN

Football came naturally to me. Being a father did not.

My eldest daughter, Erica, was born in 1987. I was introduced to her mom, Rea Ann, by Rick James, who knew all the prettiest women at the L.A. clubs. Rea Ann and I started seeing each other, but after a bit I wanted to break it off; I wanted to see other women and she wanted something more serious. Rea Ann told me she didn't care who else I saw, as long as I still saw her. She also told me she was on the pill. Neither thing was true.

I was furious—and scared. One of her girlfriends told me: *She trapped you, Eric! She* wanted *to get pregnant!* That's how it seemed to me. I was fiercely protective of my independence and I was sure I never wanted kids. I had a number of goals when I went to the NFL—making the Pro Bowl, winning a Super Bowl—and not getting a woman pregnant was one of them. When Erica was born, I wish I could say what so many dads say: *It was the greatest moment of my life.* But it wasn't. I was angry with Rea Ann and felt sorry for myself.

During the first three years of my daughter's life, I saw her two times. In short, for much of Erica's childhood, I acted like an immature asshole.

Things with Rea Ann got really ugly. Looking back, I blame myself a lot more than I blame her. She was always after me for money, even serving me court papers when I was in San Diego right after a game against the Chargers. At the time, I felt like she was torturing me—that's no overstatement of how miserable she made me—but in retrospect I see differently: she was trying to provide the best life possible for her daughter. *Our* daughter. But I fought her tooth and nail, and I wound up dragging the whole thing out a lot longer than necessary. I couldn't get past the idea that she was taking advantage of me. As an elite athlete, I'd become very sensitive to the feeling that people were using me, and that's what it felt like. I *hated* her—a consuming, unnatural hate that makes me ashamed now. I'd think crazy shit about her and say crazy shit to her. We'd get into huge, screaming fights constantly.

My mom tried to talk sense into me. *Eric! This is your child!* Both she and Helen sought out a relationship with Erica and even brought her down to Sealy. They'd send me pictures but I didn't look at them. I was angry at Rea Ann, but the real victim was Erica. My mom would tell me, *It's not that baby's fault.* But I didn't understand her and didn't want to hear it.

I came around slowly—too slowly, frankly. I started to see Erica more. I loved her and realized what a great kid she was, but I could never really see myself as a *dad*. A dad was an old man who stayed home. I was a young guy who played football and chased women.

Erica said a couple things when she was a little girl that just gutted me. One time, Rea Ann brought Erica to meet me at TGI Fridays, when Erica was three. She looked at me and asked me, *So you're my dad?*

I said I was.

She said, *So where've you been?*

The only thing I could think to say was, *I've just been away.*

Another time, when she was maybe four or five, I was walking with her when she said, *Daddy, do you love me?*

I said, *Of course I love you.*

She said, *Well, mommy says it all the time, and you never say it.*

Imagine that. A four-year-old telling a twenty-something man that it's important to express love. I made a promise to her that day that I'd tell her I loved her every time I saw her.

I'm very close with Erica now. She lives near me. She's a great person and a hard worker who juggles a demanding job with an acting, podcast, and book-writing career. She's also a great mom to her daughter, my granddaughter Irie, who's seven. But I wasn't a good father to her for most of her childhood. Despite everything, Erica didn't give up on me, and the fact that we have a great relationship today is solely because my *daughter* was the bigger person.

As time went on, things with Rea Ann and me got better: eventually, my love for Erica melted away my hatred for Rea Ann. It was impossible to sustain that hatred for so long. It was just dumb, and at a certain point I had to leave it in the past and grow up.

One day, when Erica was nineteen, she was at my house when I asked her for her mom's number. I called Rea Ann up, which was the first time in ages I'd talked to her. I could tell she was nervous on the other end, thinking I'd say something that would set off another fight. But I told her what I should have told her a long time ago: that we'd never seen eye to eye, that I was a bad co-parent, but that Erica was a smart, hardworking, good person. I said I wanted to thank her for being such a great mom to my daughter—and that I wanted her to know that *I* knew she did it in spite of me and my immaturity.

She said, *Eric, I cannot believe you're saying this.* And honestly, I couldn't believe I was saying it either. But it goes to show you how people can change.

It was a happy ending all around. Rea Ann wound up inventing a product called the Beautyblender, a simple but ingenious device for applying makeup, and Erica runs the multimillion-dollar company with her. Here's something else I can't believe I'm saying: I'm really happy for Rea Ann.

◆

Life is full of unexpected blessings. The older I get, the more I realize that sometimes the best things are the ones you didn't even think you wanted. One example is Erica. Another is the woman I love, Penny.

It was just dumb luck, another thing that happened in spite of me, not because of me. I'd been a proud bachelor my whole life and was sure settling down wasn't for me. If I was left to my own devices, I wouldn't even have met her.

It was 1999, and there was an event in Indianapolis honoring the 1987 division-winning Colts team. The way things ended there, I wasn't planning to go, but my good friends Harvey Armstrong and Jeff Herrod called me and asked me to come, and then Jim Irsay called me. I'd gotten along with Jimmy but we didn't leave off well—I'd said something publicly that wasn't so nice. It was at the height of my frustration, when it was obvious the Colts were going nowhere, and I said that Jimmy, who was general manager at the time, knew as much about being a GM as Daffy Duck did. When he called me about the reunion, he said, *Eric, this is Daffy Duck.* If he was willing to let bygones be bygones, then so was I. I decided to go.

In Indianapolis, Jeff, the former Colts linebacker, told me there was a woman he wanted me to meet: her name was Penny. She was a cool, pretty redhead. We met at a place called Club 54, and my first impression of her was that she was drop-dead gorgeous: she had once been named Miss Indiana. More important was her personality. She was assertive and sure of herself, with a good sense of humor. Plus, I could tell she fulfilled the redhead stereotype of being passionate to the point of hot-tempered, and I liked that, too.

At the club, Penny and I danced for hours. It was the most I'd ever danced before or since. She just had a good aura, someone I wanted to be around from the beginning. But at about midnight, we somehow got separated at the club for a few minutes, and when I looked for her, I learned she'd left. I was disappointed and figured I'd said something dumb and blown it. But I wanted to give it another shot, so I asked Jeff for her number and called her the next morning.

I didn't know this at the time, but Penny has a real hoarse, husky voice in the morning. When I called and she answered, I thought she was a man at first, and my heart sank.

—*Uhhh . . . is Penny there?*

—*This is Penny.*

We wound up going out that night to a Japanese steakhouse before I went back to L.A., and after that, we started talking on the phone and getting to know each other. She had a good heart, and being from Indiana, she had a wholesomeness to her that reminded me of girls back home in Texas. I could tell she was a genuine person with good values, and that she wasn't into me because I had money or was famous. She'd heard of me—her friend's mom had been a huge Colts fan—but she didn't care about any of that. I just got a good vibe from her and felt comfortable with her, like I didn't have to watch myself.

I began inviting her out to L.A., casually at first, but over time it became more serious, and at a certain point she wanted to move to L.A. full-time. One reason was her career: she designed makeup displays for department stores, and in that world, L.A. is the place to be. But the other reason was that she was ready to take our relationship to the next level.

But I wasn't. Being a bachelor had been very, very good to me, and I wasn't trying to mess with a good thing. I had Erica, and that was all the family I thought I wanted or needed. But Penny said she'd get her own place, and that sounded good to me. After she moved to L.A., we kept dating and got even closer. But then she started talking about having kids, and again I got nervous.

I love Erica more than anything, but the whole experience with Rea Ann had been exhausting, and I wasn't trying to go through something like that again. Having a kid with Penny would also tie me to her exclusively, which I wasn't ready for. At that point in my life, I was still getting out there a lot with women. I can't stress enough how protective of my independence I've always been: my folks raised me as a person who could think for himself and stand on his own two feet. I think this quality enabled me to achieve what I achieved without getting dragged down into the crap—alcohol, drugs, that do-nothing small-town mentality—that ruined so many people in Sealy. I was proud of the life I'd created and the person I was, and I didn't want anything to compromise it.

Then Penny got pregnant. That changed everything, though not immediately.

When Penny was pregnant, I became more attentive to her and we grew closer. We named our daughter Keri, after my dad, Kary.

Still, for the first three years or so of Keri's life, Penny and I were co-parents and boyfriend and girlfriend, but we still lived separately, and I didn't see Keri every day. I had my daughter but I also had my independence. That's what I thought I wanted.

But then I started to notice that on the days I wasn't with Penny and Keri, I'd miss them. That was my family; it felt weird not being with them. By that point, Penny was tired of us living separately, and she made it clear to me that the arrangement couldn't go on forever. I faced a choice: Did I want to stay on my own and possibly see another man raising my daughter with the woman I loved, or was it time to settle down?

It was an easy decision. One moment clinched it: I was spending time with Keri at Penny's place, and when I got up to leave, Keri looked up at me with her perfect child's eyes and asked, *Why are you leaving?*

Penny moved into my place soon after, and our son Dallis was born a few years later. Keri is sixteen, Dallis is ten. Penny and I aren't married, but we've been together for twenty years, so we might as well be. I realize now I'm living the life I'd wanted for a long time, even if I didn't realize it. Ever since football ended, I had felt a void, a hollowness at the center of my life that I didn't even recognize—until it was filled by my family.

Penny is the best partner a man could ask for. We play well off each other—some couples just have that, and I'm lucky that's us—and she's intuitive enough to know when I need my space. I treasure her; I don't know what I'd do without her. Now that I'm older, I realize the value of having the stability of someone by your side. If something happened to me, or my kids, she'd be there. As a parent, she's loving but stern when she needs to be. There's nothing she wouldn't do for our kids.

As a young man, I used to run around the L.A. clubs, having a good time and chasing women. Now, on weekend nights, Penny and I just curl up and watch TV, and I couldn't be happier.

♦

My days usually begin by driving Keri to school to Oaks Christian School in Westlake Village. It's just us in the car, the kind of quality time a lot of dads don't get with their kids—or, that used to be the case before she got into her phone. Keri's a kind-hearted person. Her demeanor is pretty shy, but she has a mother-hen instinct, and in school, she sticks up for people who get bullied or aren't popular. She's one of those good-hearted people who gives other people the benefit of the doubt and sometimes doesn't realize that not everyone's as kind as she is. Sometimes, I worry this quality makes her vulnerable.

She's a very gifted track runner and volleyball player, but I think her greatest talent is as a visual artist. I can't draw and neither can Penny; Keri got that talent from Penny's mom.

When Keri was in elementary school, she struggled academically: as late as fourth grade, she couldn't really read. That's when we found out she was dyslexic. Penny worked tirelessly to get her the help she needed and got her into the Westmark School, which is the best school in the area for dyslexia. An amazing teacher there, Ms. Robyn Bridges, unlocked Keri's potential and changed her life; now she gets all A's and B's. I'm proud of the grades but I'm prouder of her effort: Keri's teachers always tell me that she gives 100 percent, all the time. They tell me when something's hard for her, she doesn't quit. That makes me incredibly proud.

Dallis, who's named after my dad's brother, is inquisitive and hilarious. He has been since he was little, and some of the things he has said are legendary in our family. When he was much younger, he said to us, *When I die, I don't want them to bury me in the ground. But if they have to, could they drill a little hole, so I can breathe?*

Dallis is extremely handsome and photogenic, and has done some modeling for the Gap. Like a lot of other ten-year-old boys, he loves video games and playing sports. I'm not one of those dads who pushes sports on his kids, but Dallis is a very naturally gifted athlete—better than me, I really think. Watching some of the things he does when he's messing around, I'm blown away by how balanced and coordinated he is. I was once rubbing lotion on him when I said to myself, *Damn—this kid's muscles are cut!* He loves flag football, but he has also shown a real talent for baseball. I'd much, much rather that he gravitates to baseball, but if he wants to play football, I won't stop him.

Whatever my kids do, I know they're going to succeed, because they're strong-minded people. I always tell them what my dad told me, and I think it's rubbing off: *Whatever you do, do with your might, 'cause things done by halves are never done right.*

All those timeless values are important to me. I try to raise my kids like my parents raised me, so even though they're growing up in Calabasas, they have some Sealy in them. I take them to church every Sunday to give them a sense of perspective, because it's easy to lose that out here. I also spank them, which isn't popular these days, but a lot of kids out here don't realize that actions have consequences, which is something my kids need to know. People always tell me how well behaved and respectful my kids are.

I don't want them thinking they're better than anyone else, and I want them to know that what's important isn't what you *have* but who you *are*. Most of all, I want them to have a sense of basic fairness, which was something my mom was really big on. I remember once someone asked me: If one of my kids killed someone, would I turn them in? I said of course I would. It's something my mom taught me: nothing is more important than having a moral code and sticking to it.

My kids have a comfortable life I could've never dreamed of. They live in a big house, have all the food they need, go on all kinds of exotic vacations, and have the best educations money can buy. I try to tell them that most people don't have these things, and I tell them about my upbringing in a shotgun house where dinner was what we killed. Do they really appreciate how fortunate they are? I don't know; maybe someday they will.

Despite their privilege, they're still Black. In America, that's an inescapable fact of life, even though their mother is white. Race and racism permeates everything, even early childhood. When Keri was a little girl, a white kid in school asked her, *Why is your skin that ugly color?* When I heard about it, I tried to undo the damage—*Your skin is the most beautiful color in the world*—but some things, you can't unhear. Racism is in the air we breathe.

As the father of a Black boy, the day's coming soon when I'm gonna have to have The Talk with Dallis. I wrote about this earlier: it's a conversation my mom had with me and it's one every Black parent has with their kids. Black boys in particular need to know that as a result of their skin, the cops are on high alert, and that encounters with police can escalate in a hurry. I worry about Dallis in particular: he has a sharp tongue and a temper, just like his dad.

Fatherhood is not easy, but it's the center of my existence and I love it. On one hand, I can't believe I resisted this life for so long. On the other hand, being an older dad makes me appreciate it more.

But being an older dad has drawbacks, of course. By the time Dallis graduates from high school, for instance, I'll be seventy. I get excited about the great people they're turning into and all they're gonna accomplish, but then I get sad thinking I might not be there for a lot of it, just like my dad didn't get to see my NFL career.

My kids know this too. One time, back when Keri was little and I was walking her to school, she said to me, *Daddy, I don't want you to die.*

I told her what my dad told me. *Death is a part of life, sweetheart.* I told her to remember all the great times, the conversations, all the times we made each other laugh. I told her that I'll die and she'll die, too, but that hopefully, if we live the right way, we'll meet again.

•

There was one scary episode in particular that made me appreciate being a parent more than I otherwise would have: When Keri was six, she got very sick. It was a mysterious neurological problem and we've never quite figured out exactly what it was. But she had really bad symptoms for two years—easily the worst two years of my life.

I noticed it when we were outside, playing catch with a tennis ball, and she kept losing her balance and falling. At first I tried to dismiss it—she's tall, she's growing fast—but in the following days it became obvious that something was seriously wrong. She fell at school and busted her lip. When she'd walk, it was like an extremely drunk person walking—she'd stagger, unable to move in a straight line or find her balance. I was out of town at an event when Penny called me, and I can still hear the terror in her voice: *There's something wrong with Keri,* she said. *She's looking at me, but she's not really* looking *at me.*

I caught the next flight home. When I first saw Keri she was in the bathroom, sitting on top of the toilet seat cover with her hands in her head, just rocking back and forth. She was in pain and she was scared. That image is seared into my mind forever.

The next two years for us were spent in and out of hospitals. In and out of optimism and hopelessness. In and out of different levels of fear. We knew it was bad after we initially took her to a neurologist, and after a bunch of tests, the doctor came back to us and said: *Something's really off—but we don't know what it is.*

We went to UCLA Medical Center, L.A. Children's Hospital, and Loma Linda University Children's Hospital, which is about a hundred miles away from home. We slept on couches and juggled Keri's medical issues with the fact that Dallis was just a baby and then a toddler, and needed constant care.

I'd always heard the cliché about how when your kid is in pain, you'd rather it were you feeling the pain. That's not something you fully understand until you've been through something like this. There were so many heartbreaking moments. One time, she was eating a cookie, but her hands were shaking so badly that it was crumbling up and the pieces were going everywhere. She looked up at me and said, *I'm sorry Daddy. I'm sorry I'm wasting it.* I wanted to burst into tears.

There's nothing sadder in the world than a children's hospital. Seeing the sick kids. Seeing the parents struggle, a fate I wouldn't wish on *anybody.* I saw one mom just leave her kid in the hospital alone for days: it was all too much for her and at a certain point, she didn't have it in her to be there for him. I never did that, but I understood what she was going through.

The whole situation was frustrating as well as terrifying. Early on, I'd talked to my friend Roy Green, the former St. Louis/Phoenix Cardinals All-Pro wide receiver, and he told me his daughter had had a similar thing, and that after a while, for no apparent reason, it just went away. That gave me some hope early on, but as time went by, my dream that it would just go away—*poof!*—seemed less and less realistic.

Until, one day, it did go away—with the help of a specialist named Dr. Ayesha Zahir Sherzai at the Loma Linda Children's Hospital, and a mix of steroids and a special drug. It really seemed like a miracle. As suddenly and inexplicably as this thing came on, it went away.

Now, there are hardly any signs of it. Penny and I, since we know her so well, can see that when she gets stressed, or angry, she'll shake a little bit. But if you didn't know her you'd never notice. She's a great athlete and a great artist, so obviously the illness wasn't too debilitating.

The whole ordeal really bonded our family. Penny and I became much closer: during that time, we truly became a team, totally reliant on each other. If I was ever noncommittal about our relationship, that experience showed me why it's necessary for me to have a partner in life, and why I'm so blessed that my partner is Penny.

The experience was also a reality check for me. In many ways, being a professional athlete insulates you from reality and distorts it. But eventually you get old and you have kids and you spend nights on end in a children's hospital, and you realize that everything you once thought was important—wins and losses, the rushing record, the Heisman you should have won, even the money you spent so much of your career worrying about—doesn't mean much compared to your kid walking out of the hospital healthy.

I'm almost a senior citizen now. I'm not the young guy in the number 29 jersey from those highlight tapes, blowing past defenders for touchdowns that look pretty and easy. I'd like to think I'm something better: A man who knows what's important in life. A man who appreciates how lucky he is.

EPILOGUE

RAMBASSADOR

It still makes me sad that things didn't work out with the Rams. Even before they traded up to draft me, and I pictured myself wearing that yellow horn on my helmet, I felt they were the team I belonged with: *I'm a Ram.* Then I got out to L.A. and saw the mountains, and I saw the eclectic scene on Venice Beach, and met all the people of every color from every country and background and it felt like home. I knew in my heart that L.A. was the spot for me. But it didn't work out.

John Robinson once said that if the Rams hadn't traded me, I would've finished with 20,000 career yards behind our offensive line, which would've put the all-time rushing record out of reach. (I finished with 13,259; Emmitt Smith had 18,355). I agree with John, but that's not what bothers me. What bothers me is that we had a great thing going with those Rams teams, but the front office messed it up.

A few years after my career ended, maybe 1996 or '97, Jackie Slater called me up. He had retired from the Rams after a remarkable twenty-year career. He was close with John Shaw, who was still running things with the organization, which by then had moved to St. Louis—another thing the Rams organization did that pisses me off to this day. Jackie's a natural peacemaker, and it didn't sit well with him that the bad blood between the Rams and me had lingered. He arranged for Shaw and me to have lunch together, and we agreed to meet for a steak in Santa Monica.

The moment I sat down across from Shaw I felt my blood boiling, again: all the anger from ten years ago started coursing through me, as intense as it had ever been. It's amazing how memory works: sitting across from Shaw, I might as well have been sitting in his dingy office on Pico Boulevard, spending the hour begging him for a fair contract while he made it clear in so many words it wasn't happening.

But then Shaw apologized. He said he'd been wrong. He said he'd been young and arrogant. He made it clear he had a job to do, to protect the owner's money, and that some conflict with players was inevitable, but that he regretted how he'd treated me. He told me what I'd always felt myself: that I should've never been traded from the Rams.

By saying that, it was almost like he'd let down a shield. We had a very honest conversation after that. I told him how much all the players hated him. That my teammates and I all thought we were one player away, knocking on the door of the Super Bowl for years, but that John had cost us our shot. That I'd been angry and hurt about it ever since, and so had a lot of other guys.

John understood. And by the end of that conversation, I understood where he was coming from. We didn't go on and become best friends, and I wouldn't say there are no hard feelings. But it doesn't consume me anymore. It's like the situation with Rea Ann: it's not healthy to carry around so much bitterness.

My reconciliation with the Rams began on that day. The timing was lucky for them. Not long after that, before the 1998 draft, I came to St. Louis, where I heard the Rams were considering trading up to draft Curtis Enis, who'd been a dominant running back at Penn State. They wanted me to look at Enis and tell them what I thought.

I told them to stay away. I said Enis leaned over too much when he ran, that his legs weren't fully underneath him and that he'd get hurt. The Rams listened to me, staying put and drafting defensive end Grant Wistrom, who went on to become a key contributor to the Super Bowl–winning defense. Meanwhile, Enis blew out his knee in his second start and his career was basically over before it began.

I also helped broker the deal to get Marshall Faulk to the Rams. I'd been watching him do great things for the Colts, but his career had hit a plateau. He was a great player but that system wasn't maximizing his talent, and in the coming years, their priority was going to be developing Peyton Manning. At the time, Marshall was looking to renegotiate his contract. I was friends with Rocky Arceneaux, Marshall's agent, and I told him we could work something out to make him happy.

I called John Shaw and made the case for Marshall: the Rams needed some star power and name recognition. They needed a catalyst for the offense, the type of player who made everyone around him better. Marshall was that guy.

That set the whole thing in motion, and in the coming weeks, I was the intermediary between all the parties—the Colts, the Rams, Marshall himself—that enabled that trade to happen. The Colts got a second-rounder and a fifth-rounder. The Rams got a guy who was first-team All-Pro over the next three years and won an MVP and a Super Bowl. Without Marshall, there's no Greatest Show on Turf. There's no Rams Super Bowl season in 1999.

After the Rams won that title, the organization gave me a ring. It was a nice gesture, but it was bittersweet. I should have had more of an opportunity to win that ring as a player. And the Rams should've never left L.A.

◆

But I never left. L.A. is my city. This place is in my bones. And after my retirement, I became much more embedded in the community here. I realize how privileged I've been, and I've dedicated myself to giving back.

I launched the Eric Dickerson Foundation in 2000, which gives scholarship money to low-income kids trying to go to college. Getting out of Sealy changed my life, but I only had the opportunity because I was born with a rare talent. There are millions of talented kids out there capable of doing all kinds of great things, but they don't get the opportunity. America doesn't invest in kids from poor backgrounds; that's a tragedy and a crime. My foundation tries to help.

The foundation also runs football camps at Camp Pendleton. My friend LeRoy Irvin, the former All-Pro cornerback on our Rams teams in the '80s, got me into doing that. He'd grown up on a military base and remembered being lonely, with nothing to do. The camps are incredibly rewarding: after every one, there's always a handful of kids that come up to me and say some version of *Mr. Dickerson, I've never had so much fun in my life.*

I'm also the co-founder of the Young Warriors, an organization that pairs fatherless boys with mentors. About a decade ago, I was approached by a young man named Jason Hill, who'd grown up in a drug-infested house in Ohio but had come to L.A. and turned his life around. The stories of his childhood rattled me: he said his mom was a drug addict, and that he had no idea who his dad was because his *mom* had no idea who his dad was. As a kid, he'd wake up in the morning and climb over ten passed-out addicts sleeping on the floor of his house. Several years before we met, his sister had died of an overdose.

My biological dad had left too, but I was lucky to be raised by a great father. But when he died when I was seventeen, I got a small taste of the directionlessness that so many kids feel. Jason and I visited the California City Correctional Facility, where I learned that children growing up without fathers are twice as likely to wind up incarcerated as those from homes with a mom and dad. It makes sense: if a boy isn't modeling himself after his dad, there's a good chance he's modeling himself after the drug dealer on the corner. Fathers are absolutely essential—and knowing this makes me regret being absent for a lot of Erica's childhood.

Every year, I host a golf tournament to raise funds for the Young Warriors. I've developed a broad network of people who contribute money. In a city like L.A., it's easy to move in rich and glamorous circles. But there's so much poverty, so much need, so much inequality, so much injustice. The work I do with my foundation and the Young Warriors is rewarding. And like the quest for social and racial justice in America, it's also unending.

•

The Rams came back to L.A. in 2016, finally doing right by the city they'd betrayed in the '90s. That they came back to L.A. itself, and not Orange County, is significant.

Then, they did right by me: in 2017, I signed a ceremonial one-day contract and "retired" as a Ram. It was just a gesture, but a meaningful one.

That year, I also accepted a job as the Rams' vice president of business development. In my role, I'm constantly interacting with the fans, which I really enjoy. During my playing career, my public persona was dictated by the media. I saw the things they wrote—that I was a *malcontent*, an *ingrate*, a *bad teammate*—and I'd get frustrated, because I always knew that wasn't me. When I'd try to defend myself to the writers, everything I'd say was used against me, and they'd always make me look even worse. Eventually I gave up trying. The writers would write what they would write, and it was out of my hands.

But when I went out into L.A., I noticed something: despite how the press portrayed me, the vast majority of fans really liked me. I had a really good rapport with them. I came to realize that L.A. is a really big place: the racist hate mail I got, and the fans who threw fake money at me at Anaheim Stadium, represented a tiny minority. For everyone else, it's been a lovefest since 1983. I've always gone out of my way to be accessible. When someone asks me for my autograph, I feel honored. I know I'm blessed to be in the position where I hold such a significant place in people's minds. I've never lost sight of that and I've tried my hardest not to let people down, even if it has meant signing autographs for hours, when I was dead-tired and hurting. These days, I'll pose for any selfie anyone wants to take with me.

The "long story short" is that when it comes to my relationship with the fans, reality on the ground didn't match the perception of me in the media.

That's been apparent since I've started working for the Rams. They call me the "Rambassador." I consider myself the voice of the fans. They know I'll always tell the truth, even though I work for the organization. They know I'm not afraid to ruffle feathers.

The year before the Rams hired me, I butted heads with Jeff Fisher, who was in the process of coaching the team to five straight sub-.500 seasons, from 2012 until he was fired in 2016. That year, the Rams' first season back in L.A., I criticized the team and Fisher, saying the losing had to stop. Considering the passion we played with in the '80s, the flat version of the Rams that came back to L.A. in 2016 was not acceptable.

Fisher got pissed. He called me on the phone and said that if I criticized the team, I couldn't stand on the sidelines during games anymore.

He shouldn't have started with me. Our beef spilled out into the public. The fans took my side, overwhelmingly. It wasn't a hard choice: the greatest player in franchise history or the coach who'd never had a winning season?

Soon after, Fisher was fired. Then the Rams hired me for my current position.

Even though I work for the organization, I'm not the type to toe the company line. That happened when Aaron Donald—easily the greatest defensive player in the game today—was holding out for a new contract. Having once been in Aaron's shoes, I publicly took his side.

I was also vocal about my disdain for the Rams' new uniforms. Uniforms have always meant a lot to me: the old Rams uniforms were a big reason why I wanted to come here in the first place. But the new uniforms are soft—and I said so after the design was unveiled. I'd seen people say that the secondary logo, of a ram's head, looked like a penis—and I agreed with that statement. The whole thing got a lot of attention on social media and even turned into an impromptu fundraiser the Rams organized: in exchange for the opportunity to get to hear team COO Kevin Demoff read mean tweets about the uniforms on camera, the fans raised more than $2.3 million for charity.

All of this goes to say that in many ways, my second stint as a Rams employee has been more fun than the first. In addition to my work with the Rams, I'm also a football analyst for Fox Sports 1, and

I do two radio shows with iHeartRadio. Back in the day, I bristled at how I was presented to the public. Now I get to be myself and speak from the heart, and it feels good.

It feels good because I think I have something to say. I've lived through a lot. I went from a shotgun shack on a dirt road in Texas to a big house in the hills of Calabasas. I achieved the American Dream—but I saw the underside that nobody wants to talk about. I was born as a Black boy in the segregated South, but the most severe racism I experienced occurred after I became an NFL star. I took the SMU program to new heights, then became the guy everyone blames for its downfall. I set NFL records while making it look pretty and easy, but now I can't get a good night's sleep and I worry about my battered body and brain. I love football, but a part of me despises it. I live with that tension every day: the sport that defines me, that gave me some of the best moments of my life and the privilege my kids enjoy now, has also made me feel so unhappy and so mistreated.

It's a life nobody would've imagined for a child conceived in the back of a car by two teenagers. It's a life I wouldn't have dreamed of when I was in seventh grade, wearing prescription glasses under my helmet, terrified of getting tackled in my first ever organized football game. But it's my life, and this is my story.

ABOUT HAYMARKET BOOKS

Haymarket Books is a radical, independent, nonprofit book publisher based in Chicago.

Our mission is to publish books that contribute to struggles for social and economic justice. We strive to make our books a vibrant and organic part of social movements and the education and development of a critical, engaged, international left.

We take inspiration and courage from our namesakes, the Haymarket martyrs, who gave their lives fighting for a better world. Their 1886 struggle for the eight-hour day—which gave us May Day, the international workers' holiday—reminds workers around the world that ordinary people can organize and struggle for their own liberation. These struggles continue today across the globe—struggles against oppression, exploitation, poverty, and war.

Since our founding in 2001, Haymarket Books has published more than five hundred titles. Radically independent, we seek to drive a wedge into the risk-averse world of corporate book publishing. Our authors include Noam Chomsky, Arundhati Roy, Rebecca Solnit, Angela Y. Davis, Howard Zinn, Amy Goodman, Wallace Shawn, Mike Davis, Winona LaDuke, Ilan Pappé, Richard Wolff, Dave Zirin, Keeanga-Yamahtta Taylor, Nick Turse, Dahr Jamail, David Barsamian, Elizabeth Laird, Amira Hass, Mark Steel, Avi Lewis, Naomi Klein, and Neil Davidson. We are also the trade publishers of the acclaimed Historical Materialism Book Series and of Dispatch Books.